Poveglia Island: Haunting Secrets of Italy's Most Terrifying Haunted Destination

Oliver Lancaster

Published by Oliver Lancaster, 2023.

While every precaution has been taken in the preparation of this book, the publisher assumes no responsibility for errors or omissions, or for damages resulting from the use of the information contained herein.

POVEGLIA ISLAND: HAUNTING SECRETS OF ITALY'S MOST TERRIFYING HAUNTED DESTINATION

First edition. July 26, 2023.

ISBN: 979-8223671015

Written by Oliver Lancaster.

Also by Oliver Lancaster

Chernobyl: Unveiling the tragedy. A Comprehensive Account of the Nuclear Disaster

The Bhopal Gas Tragedy: Unraveling the Catastrophe of 1984

The Deepwater Horizon Oil Spill of 2010: A Disaster Unveiled

Fukushima Fallout: Unveiling the Truth behind the 2011 Nuclear Disaster

Minamata Disease: Poisoned Waters and the Battle for Justice (1932-1968)

Evil Women: Unmasking History's Most Notorious Women

Bundy The Dark Chronicles: America's Infamous Serial Killer

Dahmer The Dark Chronicles: America's Infamous Milwaukee Cannibal

Zodiac The Dark Chronicles: America's Infamous Cryptic Killer

Bigfoot: The Comprehensive Investigation into the Elusive Legend

Chasing Legends: The Truth behind the Chupacabra

Chasing Legends: The Truth behind the Loch Ness Monster

Aokigahara Forest: The Heartbreaking Secrets of Japan's Suicide Forest

The Amityville House: The Haunting Secrets of America's Most Infamous Residence

The Stanley Hotel: The Mystery of Colorado's Historic Landmark
The Tower of London: The Haunted Past and Secrets of Royal Ghosts
The Winchester Mystery House: The Riddle of Sarah Winchester's Mansion
Vanished Skies: The Mysterious Disappearance of Amelia Earhart
Vanishing Point: The Bermuda Triangle Exposed
Poveglia Island: Haunting Secrets of Italy's Most Terrifying Haunted Destination
Tracing Footsteps: The Mystery of Madeleine McCann

Watch for more at https://tinyurl.com/olanc.

Table of Contents

Sign up to my free newsletter to get updates on new releases, FREE teaser chapters to upcoming releases and FREE digital short stories.

Or visit https://tinyurl.com/olanc

I never spam and you can unsubscribe at any time.

OLIVER LANCASTER

Disclaimer

The information presented in this book is based on historical records, eyewitness accounts, paranormal investigations, and folklore associated with Poveglia Island. While every effort has been made to ensure accuracy, the author and publisher do not claim the validity of supernatural claims or personal experiences mentioned herein. Readers are encouraged to approach the subject matter with an open mind and understand that belief in the paranormal is a matter of personal interpretation.

Poveglia Island: Haunting Secrets of Italy's Most Terrifying Haunted Destination

Chapter 1: The Enigmatic Island's Origins

Poveglia Island, situated in the Venetian Lagoon, off the northeastern coast of Italy, is a place steeped in both beauty and darkness. Its geological and geographical characteristics have played a crucial role in shaping its unique history, making it a captivating yet chilling destination.

Poveglia Island, like much of the Venetian Lagoon, owes its existence to the complex geological processes that took place over millennia. The island's formation began with the deposition of sediments brought by rivers flowing into the lagoon, gradually building up land masses. The interactions between tides, currents, and sedimentation resulted in the emergence of numerous islands, including Poveglia.

Poveglia Island covers an area of approximately 7.5 hectares, making it one of the smaller islands in the Venetian Lagoon. Its topography is relatively flat, with the highest point reaching just a few meters above sea level. This characteristic made the island susceptible to frequent flooding during high tides and storm surges, posing challenges to any potential settlements throughout history.

The island's strategic location within the Venetian Lagoon made it an important outpost during the Roman and Byzantine periods. Its proximity to the bustling city of Venice made it an ideal point for defense and surveillance, as well as a convenient stop for sailors and traders. However, its advantageous location also made it vulnerable to invasions and pirate raids throughout the centuries.

Historical records suggest that Poveglia Island was inhabited as early as the 5th century. It was likely first settled by those seeking refuge from barbarian invasions on the nearby mainland. Over time, the island's population grew, and it became home to various communities that engaged in fishing, farming, and salt production. Despite these early settlements, Poveglia remained relatively rural and less developed than its neighboring islands.

Poveglia Island's darkest chapter in history began during the outbreak of the bubonic plague in the 14th century. As the plague ravaged Europe, the Venetian Republic used the island as a quarantine station for ships arriving from plague-infested regions. This move was an attempt to contain the spread of the deadly disease within the city of Venice itself. Unfortunately, this decision would lead to a haunting legacy that still permeates the island today.

In the 16th century, during the height of the plague epidemic, the Venetian government took a more drastic step in its efforts to isolate the infected. They constructed a hospital on Poveglia Island to house and treat those suffering from the plague. This hospital, known as the "Lazzaretto," became a grim place where thousands of plague victims lived out their final, painful days.

As the plague-infested ships arrived on the island, those showing symptoms of the disease were immediately taken to the hospital, while others were forcibly separated from their families, never to be seen again. The vast number of deaths and the manner in which they occurred contributed to the island's eerie reputation.

After the plague outbreak subsided, Poveglia Island continued to serve as a quarantine station during subsequent outbreaks. In the 20th century, the island was once again utilized during the outbreak of the bubonic plague and later as a mental health facility. The asylum, constructed in the early 1920s, added another dark layer to Poveglia's history, with rumors of cruel experiments and mistreatment of patients.

Today, Poveglia Island stands abandoned, its buildings in ruins, and its chilling past echoing through the decaying structures. The geological and geographical characteristics that once made it strategically important now serve as a backdrop to the haunting secrets that lie within its soil and crumbling walls.

1. Roman and Byzantine Influence:

POVEGLIA ISLAND'S HISTORY traces back to the Roman and Byzantine periods, where it played a strategic role within the Venetian Lagoon. As a part of the Venetian Republic, the island served as an outpost for defense and surveillance. Its geographical location, being close to the thriving city of Venice, made it a convenient stopping point for sailors and traders traveling through the lagoon.

During this era, Poveglia likely saw the establishment of small settlements, driven by the need for refuge from invading forces on the mainland. These early inhabitants engaged in fishing, farming, and salt production, forming the foundations of the island's rural lifestyle.

2. Poveglia and the Plague:

THE MOST SIGNIFICANT and haunting chapter of Poveglia Island's history began in the 14th century with the outbreak of the bubonic plague, also known as the Black Death. As the deadly disease spread across Europe, the Venetian Republic took measures to protect the city of Venice, including the establishment of quarantine stations for incoming ships.

Poveglia Island, with its isolation and suitable location, became an ideal quarantine destination. Ships suspected of carrying plague-infected individuals were required to dock at the island. Those showing symptoms of the disease were taken to the Lazzaretto, the hospital constructed on Poveglia, to be treated or isolated. Tragically, many never left the island alive.

The sheer number of deaths and the haunting manner in which they occurred shaped the island's identity, creating a dark and eerie reputation that persists to this day. The suffering and loss experienced during the plague outbreaks left an indelible mark on Poveglia, influencing its character and folklore for centuries to come.

3. The Lazzaretto and Later Uses:

FOLLOWING THE PLAGUE outbreaks, Poveglia Island continued to serve as a quarantine station during subsequent waves of the disease. In the 16th century, the Venetian government constructed a permanent Lazzaretto, signaling the island's role as a place of containment and isolation.

In the early 20th century, Poveglia's history took yet another dark turn when the island was used as a mental health facility. The asylum, built in the 1920s, housed patients with various mental illnesses, and stories of mistreatment and cruel experiments emerged, further adding to the island's grim reputation.

4. Abandonment and Present Day:

OVER TIME, ADVANCEMENTS in medical understanding and treatment led to the closure of the mental health facility on Poveglia Island. Since then, the island has been largely abandoned, with its buildings falling into ruin and nature slowly reclaiming the land.

Today, Poveglia stands as a ghostly reminder of its troubled past. Its identity is deeply intertwined with the horrors of the plague, the suffering of patients in the mental asylum, and the eerie stories that have been passed down through generations. Despite its haunting past, Poveglia Island has also become a subject of fascination for ghost hunters, paranormal enthusiasts, and those intrigued by its chilling history.

The early civilizations' interactions with Poveglia Island have significantly shaped its identity over time. From being a strategic outpost during the Roman and Byzantine periods to becoming a place of suffering and death during the plague outbreaks, and later, a site of controversial mental health practices, Poveglia's history is a reflection of humanity's triumphs and darker moments. Its past continues to capture the imagination of those who dare to explore its haunted secrets, making it Italy's most terrifying and enigmatic destination.

POVEGLIA ISLAND: HAUNTING SECRETS OF ITALY'S MOST TERRIFYING HAUNTED DESTINATION

13

Chapter 2: A Dark Past Unearthed

The bubonic plague, one of the deadliest pandemics in human history, swept through Europe multiple times, leaving death and devastation in its wake. Among the regions affected was the Venetian Republic, and Poveglia Island played a crucial role as a quarantine site during these plague outbreaks. Historical documents and reports offer valuable insights into the island's involvement in containing the spread of the disease.

One of the earliest mentions of Poveglia Island's role in handling plague outbreaks can be traced back to the 14th century. The Venetian Senate issued a decree in response to the Black Death, ordering that ships arriving in Venice from plague-affected areas should anchor at Poveglia for a period of 40 days (hence the term "quarantine," derived from "quaranta giorni" meaning "40 days" in Italian).

The decree aimed to isolate potential carriers of the disease, giving rise to the concept of quarantine, which is still used today in public health emergencies. Historical records indicate that during this period, Poveglia became a focal point for screening incoming ships and passengers, and those suspected of carrying the plague were held on the island for observation.

As the plague outbreaks persisted, the Venetian authorities recognized the need for a more permanent and designated quarantine facility on Poveglia Island. In the mid-16th century, they constructed a hospital known as the Lazzaretto, which became instrumental in the quarantine efforts.

Reports from that era reveal that the Lazzaretto was designed to accommodate a large number of individuals, with separate wards for the sick and the healthy. The hospital was equipped to provide basic medical care, but the conditions were often squalid and overcrowded, exacerbating the suffering of those already afflicted by the disease.

Contemporary reports from travelers and officials shed light on the grim realities faced by those placed in quarantine on Poveglia Island. The conditions were dire, with limited access to food, clean water, and proper sanitation. The fear of contracting the plague and the prospect of never leaving the island alive weighed heavily on the minds of those held there.

There are accounts of families being forcibly separated, with individuals showing no symptoms of the disease still being quarantined to prevent potential outbreaks. The psychological toll of isolation, combined with the physical suffering, made Poveglia a place of despair and hopelessness for those trapped there.

As plague outbreaks subsided and medical knowledge advanced, the use of Poveglia Island as a quarantine site diminished. However, its association with the bubonic plague has left an enduring legacy, contributing to the island's haunted reputation.

The memory of the suffering and death experienced during those dark times has been passed down through generations,

POVEGLIA ISLAND: HAUNTING SECRETS OF ITALY'S MOST TERRIFYING HAUNTED DESTINATION

fueling chilling tales of ghosts and malevolent spirits haunting the abandoned buildings. Poveglia's role as a quarantine site during the plague outbreaks is a reminder of the fragility of human existence and the immense impact of infectious diseases on history.

Historical documents and reports provide a glimpse into Poveglia Island's significant role as a quarantine site during the bubonic plague outbreaks in the region. From the early use of temporary quarantine measures to the construction of the permanent Lazzaretto hospital, the island became a focal point in the Venetian Republic's efforts to contain the deadly disease. The haunting memories of those dark times continue to shape Poveglia's identity as one of Italy's most terrifying haunted destinations.

During the bubonic plague outbreaks in the Venetian Republic, Poveglia Island served as a quarantine site for those suspected or confirmed to be carrying the disease. The methods employed to isolate and treat plague victims on the island had a profound impact on its reputation, shaping its identity as a place of suffering and despair.

Plague outbreaks were met with fear and panic, and authorities believed that isolation was the most effective method to prevent the spread of the disease. Ships arriving in Venice from plague-affected regions were forcibly directed to Poveglia Island, where passengers and crew members underwent a mandatory quarantine period.

The forced isolation, while intended to contain the spread of the plague, contributed to a sense of despair and hopelessness among those held on the island. Families were separated, and individuals were torn away from their loved ones without any guarantee of reuniting. This enforced quarantine gave rise to tales of anguish and sorrow, adding to the island's haunting reputation.

The establishment of the Lazzaretto hospital on Poveglia Island represented a more permanent and designated approach to treating plague victims. The hospital was designed to accommodate a large number of patients and was equipped to provide basic medical care. However, conditions in the hospital were far from ideal, with overcrowding, limited resources, and inadequate sanitation.

Plague victims who were taken to the Lazzaretto faced a harsh and grim reality. The suffering endured by patients and the high mortality rate within the hospital further added to the island's dark reputation. Instead of being a place of healing and hope, the Lazzaretto became synonymous with death and suffering, contributing to the island's aura of malevolence.

Historical accounts suggest that during times of severe plague outbreaks, desperate measures were taken to contain the disease. There are reports of bodies being disposed of in mass graves on Poveglia Island to prevent further contamination. Such practices, while driven by the need to control the epidemic, added to the island's macabre atmosphere.

POVEGLIA ISLAND: HAUNTING SECRETS OF ITALY'S MOST TERRIFYING HAUNTED DESTINATION

In later years, when the island was used as a mental health facility, controversial treatment methods and rumors of cruel experiments further darkened Poveglia's reputation. The convergence of these disturbing practices over the centuries contributed to a pervasive sense of horror and intrigue surrounding the island.

The methods used to isolate and treat plague victims on Poveglia Island left a lasting impact on its reputation. The suffering, death, and fear experienced by those who were quarantined or treated there became woven into the fabric of the island's identity.

As the centuries passed, stories of the island's haunting past were passed down through generations, solidifying its reputation as a place of tragedy and malevolence. The enduring legacy of the bubonic plague and the island's role in containing it contributed to Poveglia's status as one of Italy's most terrifying haunted destinations.

The methods used to isolate and treat plague victims on Poveglia Island had a profound impact on its reputation. Forced quarantine, the establishment of the Lazzaretto, and controversial practices all contributed to the island's identity as a place of suffering, death, and despair. The haunting memories of these dark times continue to fuel the chilling tales and folklore surrounding Poveglia, cementing its status as a haunting destination with a history tainted by the horrors of the past.

Chapter 3: The Haunting of Poveglia's Asylum

In the early 20th century, Poveglia Island underwent another transformation when it became home to a mental hospital. The asylum was established to house and treat individuals with mental illnesses, but the treatment of mentally ill patients during its operation was marred by controversy and alleged cruelty, adding another dark chapter to the island's already haunting history.

The decision to build a mental hospital on Poveglia Island was part of a broader initiative by the Italian government to address the growing issue of mental health care. In the early 1920s, the hospital was constructed to provide treatment for individuals suffering from various psychiatric disorders. The hospital's remote location on the island was seen as an advantage, as it allowed for the isolation of the mentally ill patients from the mainland population.

As the mental hospital began admitting patients, issues of overcrowding and poor living conditions quickly surfaced. The facilities were not adequately equipped to handle the growing number of patients, resulting in cramped and unsanitary conditions. Patients were often housed in dilapidated buildings that had once served as quarantine wards during the plague outbreaks, exacerbating the grim atmosphere of the hospital.

Reports from the time suggest that the hospital staff struggled to provide proper care and treatment to the patients due to the lack of resources and overcrowding. As a result, many patients were left to languish in neglect, with little access to adequate medical care or mental health treatments.

During its operation, the mental hospital on Poveglia Island employed controversial treatment methods, many of which were considered outdated and inhumane even by the standards of that era. It is alleged that patients were subjected to harsh and unproven treatments, including electroconvulsive therapy and lobotomies.

Lobotomies, in particular, were performed on some patients as a means of attempting to control their behavior. This highly invasive procedure involved severing connections in the brain's prefrontal cortex, often with devastating consequences for the patients' cognitive and emotional functioning.

Over time, disturbing rumors emerged about the treatment of patients on Poveglia Island. There are accounts of hospital staff engaging in cruel and abusive behavior towards the mentally ill patients. Patients were reportedly restrained for extended periods, subjected to physical abuse, and isolated from one another, further exacerbating their suffering.

Such reports of mistreatment contributed to the island's reputation as a place of horror and despair, perpetuating the chilling stories and folklore associated with Poveglia.

The Poveglia mental hospital's troubled history eventually caught the attention of the public and the Italian government.

POVEGLIA ISLAND: HAUNTING SECRETS OF ITALY'S MOST TERRIFYING HAUNTED DESTINATION

Amid mounting criticism and growing awareness of the poor conditions and controversial practices, the hospital was closed in the 1960s.

After its closure, Poveglia Island was left abandoned, with the buildings falling into disrepair. The echoes of its dark past continued to haunt the island, drawing the fascination of ghost hunters and paranormal enthusiasts.

Today, Poveglia Island remains largely uninhabited, with its mental hospital in ruins. While there have been proposals for its redevelopment or transformation into a tourist destination, the island's grim history continues to cast a shadow over any potential plans.

The establishment and operation of the mental hospital on Poveglia Island represent a disturbing period in the treatment of mental illness. The overcrowded and unsanitary conditions, coupled with controversial and inhumane treatment methods, have contributed to the island's chilling reputation as a place of suffering, cruelty, and paranormal activity.

The establishment of the mental hospital on Poveglia Island marked another dark phase in its history. The treatment of mentally ill patients during its operation was marked by overcrowding, poor conditions, and the use of controversial and inhumane methods. The legacy of mistreatment and neglect has solidified Poveglia's identity as a place of horror and tragedy, perpetuating its reputation as Italy's most terrifying haunted destination.

The alleged experiments and cruel practices that took place within the walls of the mental asylum on Poveglia Island are some of the most disturbing aspects of its dark history. While historical documentation and official records are scarce, numerous chilling stories and testimonies from former staff and patients have surfaced over the years, painting a haunting picture of the mistreatment endured by vulnerable individuals in the asylum.

Lobotomies were among the most infamous and controversial procedures performed on mentally ill patients at the Poveglia asylum. This procedure involved severing or damaging the frontal lobes of the brain, with the aim of controlling severe mental illness or aggressive behavior. However, the procedure was often conducted without adequate medical evaluation or proper consent, resulting in irreversible damage and significant side effects for many patients.

It is alleged that the mental hospital's staff performed numerous lobotomies, subjecting patients to this invasive and unproven treatment without regard for their well-being or the long-term consequences.

Electroconvulsive therapy, also known as electroshock therapy, was another controversial treatment method employed within the asylum. ECT involves administering an electric shock to the brain, inducing a controlled seizure with the intention of alleviating severe psychiatric conditions.

While ECT can be an effective treatment for certain mental disorders when administered under strict medical guidelines, reports suggest that on Poveglia Island, the therapy was administered indiscriminately and without proper oversight. Patients were allegedly subjected to frequent and excessive ECT sessions, leading to severe physical and emotional trauma.

The asylum's overcrowded and unsanitary conditions also contributed to the suffering of patients. Reports indicate that the hospital was ill-equipped to accommodate the growing number of mentally ill individuals. Patients were often crammed into dilapidated buildings, lacking basic amenities and proper sanitation.

The lack of adequate care and living conditions only worsened the mental and physical health of the patients, further deepening their anguish and despair.

Disturbing accounts of physical and psychological abuse perpetrated by the asylum's staff have been recounted by former patients and employees. Patients were reportedly subjected to restraint and confinement for prolonged periods, exacerbating their sense of helplessness and isolation.

Verbal abuse and humiliation were also alleged, with some staff members resorting to cruel and degrading treatment of the patients. Such acts of mistreatment left a lasting impact on the victims, perpetuating the cycle of fear and suffering within the asylum's walls.

One of the most distressing aspects of the alleged experiments and cruel practices at the Poveglia asylum was the lack of proper oversight and accountability. The isolated location of the island and the prevailing attitudes toward mental illness at the time allowed such abuses to go unchecked.

The absence of stringent regulations and oversight mechanisms meant that the vulnerable patients in the asylum were left at the mercy of their caregivers, leading to widespread exploitation and mistreatment.

In conclusion, the alleged experiments and cruel practices that took place within the walls of the mental asylum on Poveglia Island reflect a dark period in the history of mental health care. Lobotomies, electroconvulsive therapy, unsanitary living conditions, and abusive treatment contributed to the suffering and despair endured by mentally ill patients. The lack of oversight and accountability allowed such cruelty to persist, leaving a chilling legacy that continues to haunt the island's reputation as a place of horror and tragedy.

POVEGLIA ISLAND: HAUNTING SECRETS OF ITALY'S MOST TERRIFYING HAUNTED DESTINATION

Chapter 4: Forbidden Island: Poveglia's Inaccessibility

Poveglia Island is in a state of disrepair, with many of its buildings in ruins and unstable structures. As a result, the island poses significant safety risks to anyone attempting to visit without proper authorization. The decaying structures and the unstable terrain could lead to accidents, such as building collapses or injuries from falling debris.

Additionally, due to the island's haunting reputation and dark history, there is a concern that thrill-seekers or paranormal enthusiasts might attempt to explore the island without considering the safety hazards. To protect the public from potential accidents and injuries, access to Poveglia is restricted.

Poveglia Island is of historical and cultural significance, with ties to the plague outbreaks and the mental hospital's dark past. To preserve the island's historical heritage and prevent further deterioration, access is limited to authorized personnel or researchers who may be conducting studies or restoration efforts.

Unauthorized visitors could inadvertently cause damage to the already fragile structures, disrupt potential archaeological sites, or disturb historical artifacts. Restricting access helps protect the island's historical value and allows for proper conservation measures to be implemented.

In addition to its historical importance, Poveglia Island is also an essential habitat for various plant and animal species. The island's natural ecosystems have developed over time, and unrestricted access could lead to environmental damage or disturbance to the flora and fauna.

By restricting access, the authorities aim to protect the delicate balance of the island's ecosystems, allowing nature to flourish undisturbed.

Poveglia Island's reputation as one of Italy's most haunted destinations has fueled numerous supernatural legends and ghost stories. The island's eerie history attracts thrill-seekers and ghost hunters, who may attempt to access the island for paranormal investigations.

To deter unauthorized entry and prevent potential disturbances or vandalism, access restrictions are strictly enforced. This also helps preserve the peace and privacy of the island for those who genuinely seek to study its history or conduct legitimate research.

From a legal perspective, unauthorized entry onto Poveglia Island can be considered trespassing. Any accidents or injuries that occur as a result of unauthorized entry could result in legal liability for both the visitors and the authorities responsible for the island's management.

To avoid legal complications and potential harm to visitors, stringent access controls are in place.

Measures to Prevent Unauthorized Entry:

TO ENFORCE RESTRICTED access to Poveglia Island, the authorities have implemented various measures, including:

- Regular patrols by law enforcement or security personnel to deter trespassers.

- Fencing and barriers around the island's perimeter to prevent physical entry.

- Signs and warnings indicating that the island is off-limits to the public.

- Surveillance cameras to monitor any attempted unauthorized entry.

- Coordination with local authorities and law enforcement to enforce access restrictions.

It is crucial to respect access restrictions to Poveglia Island for the preservation of its historical, cultural, and natural heritage, as well as for public safety. If you are interested in visiting the island or conducting research, it is essential to seek the necessary permissions and approvals from the relevant authorities.

Preserving Poveglia Island's history while keeping it off-limits to the public presents numerous challenges for the authorities involved in its management and conservation. Balancing the need to protect the island's historical, cultural, and natural heritage with the public's curiosity and interest in its haunting past is a delicate task that requires thoughtful planning and management. Some of the challenges faced by authorities in preserving the island's history while restricting public access include:

1. Deterioration and Structural Instability:

Poveglia Island's buildings and structures are in a state of disrepair and are susceptible to deterioration due to exposure to the elements over the years. The lack of regular maintenance and upkeep, combined with the island's abandoned condition, has resulted in structural instability and safety hazards. Preserving the historical significance of the island requires protecting its architectural heritage, but allowing public access without proper safety measures could exacerbate the deterioration and put visitors at risk.

2. Protection from Vandalism and Theft:

The island's haunting reputation has attracted thrill-seekers, vandals, and even treasure hunters who may attempt to gain unauthorized entry. Protecting Poveglia from vandalism, theft of historical artifacts, and graffiti poses a significant challenge for the authorities. Any unauthorized tampering with the island's historical structures and artifacts can irreversibly damage its cultural heritage.

3. Environmental Conservation:

Poveglia Island is not only historically significant but also serves as a natural ecosystem supporting various plant and animal species. Balancing the preservation of its natural habitats with access restrictions is crucial to safeguarding its ecological value. Unrestricted public access could lead to trampling of sensitive vegetation, disturbance to wildlife, and degradation of natural habitats.

4. Managing Public Interest and Curiosity:

Poveglia's haunting history and legends have captured the public's imagination, leading to a strong curiosity about the island. Managing public interest while keeping the island off-limits can be challenging, as unauthorized attempts to visit the island may still occur, despite access restrictions. Addressing the public's fascination with the island's history while adhering to preservation efforts is an ongoing task.

5. Balancing Research and Conservation Needs:

While preserving the island's history and heritage is crucial, allowing researchers and historians access for studies and documentation is equally important. Striking a balance between research needs and access restrictions can be complex. Researchers can contribute valuable insights into the island's history, but granting access must be carefully managed to avoid damage to fragile structures and the environment.

6. Funding and Resources:

Preserving Poveglia Island requires financial resources for conservation efforts, safety measures, and ongoing maintenance. Securing sufficient funding can be challenging, especially if the island is not open to the public for tourism or other commercial activities.

7. Long-Term Sustainability:

Ensuring the long-term sustainability of conservation efforts and access restrictions is a challenge that requires commitment from relevant authorities and stakeholders. Maintaining the island's historical and natural heritage for future generations requires ongoing planning and investment.

Preserving Poveglia Island's history while keeping it off-limits to the public is a multifaceted challenge. The authorities must carefully balance the need to protect the island's historical, cultural, and natural significance with managing public curiosity and interest. Effective conservation efforts, safety measures, and careful management of access are crucial to ensure that Poveglia's haunting history endures while safeguarding its integrity for future generations.

POVEGLIA ISLAND: HAUNTING SECRETS OF ITALY'S MOST TERRIFYING HAUNTED DESTINATION

Chapter 5: The Ghostly Encounters

Analyzing accounts of visitors who claim to have experienced paranormal activities on Poveglia Island can provide valuable insights into the island's haunting reputation and the enduring fascination with its dark history. It's important to note that these accounts are subjective and not scientifically verifiable, but they offer a glimpse into the psychological and emotional impact the island's legends have on those who dare to explore it.

Many visitors report feeling an overwhelming sense of foreboding and unease as soon as they set foot on Poveglia Island. The island's desolate and decaying structures, combined with its history of suffering and death, contribute to a haunting atmosphere. Visitors often describe feeling as if they are being watched or surrounded by an unseen presence, heightening their sense of anxiety and trepidation.

Accounts often include reports of unexplained noises such as footsteps, moans, and whispers coming from empty rooms or dark corners. Some visitors claim to have witnessed shadowy figures or apparitions moving through the abandoned buildings. These experiences evoke a sense of the supernatural and reinforce the island's reputation as a paranormal hotspot.

Several visitors mention sudden drops in temperature and unexplained fluctuations in electronic devices, including cameras and flashlights. Batteries draining rapidly, despite being fully charged, are a common theme. Such occurrences are often associated with paranormal phenomena and can heighten the feeling of being in the presence of something unexplainable.

Some accounts describe visitors feeling as though they were being touched or pushed by unseen forces. These physical sensations can be particularly unsettling and contribute to a heightened sense of fear and vulnerability during the exploration.

Visitors often describe experiencing strong emotional responses during their time on Poveglia Island. These may include feelings of sadness, despair, or even anger. Many visitors report feeling overwhelmed with emotions that seem to emanate from the island's tragic history, creating a profound connection to the past and the suffering that occurred there.

Several accounts mention a sense of losing track of time or experiencing disorientation while on the island. This phenomenon is sometimes attributed to the island's haunting energy, which may affect visitors' perceptions and cognitive processing.

One striking aspect of the accounts is that multiple visitors often report similar experiences independently of each other. These shared experiences, such as hearing the same noises or witnessing the same apparitions, lend credibility to the claims and contribute to the island's reputation as a place of genuine paranormal activity.

POVEGLIA ISLAND: HAUNTING SECRETS OF ITALY'S MOST TERRIFYING HAUNTED DESTINATION

The accounts of visitors who claim to have experienced paranormal activities on Poveglia Island reflect the enduring fascination with its haunting history. The reported feelings of unease, unexplained noises, apparitions, and unusual occurrences contribute to the island's chilling reputation as one of Italy's most terrifying haunted destinations. While these accounts may not be scientifically verifiable, they provide a fascinating insight into the power of folklore and the human imagination in shaping our perception of haunted places.

Based on the reported ghostly encounters on Poveglia Island, we can categorize them into different types of paranormal phenomena. While these encounters are subjective and not scientifically verified, they align with common categories of ghostly experiences reported in haunted locations worldwide. The reported types of phenomena include:

1. Apparitions: Visitors have reported witnessing shadowy figures or full-bodied apparitions moving through the abandoned buildings on Poveglia Island. These spectral forms are often described as fleeting and elusive, adding to the eerie atmosphere of the place.

2. Voices and Whispers: Many accounts mention hearing unexplained voices, whispers, moans, or other eerie sounds emanating from empty rooms or dark corners. These disembodied voices are often indistinct, contributing to the unsettling feeling of being surrounded by unseen entities.

3. Unexplained Noises: Visitors have reported hearing footsteps, banging sounds, and other unexplained noises that cannot be attributed to natural causes. These auditory phenomena add to the sense of the supernatural and heighten feelings of fear and uncertainty.

4. Cold Spots and Temperature Changes: Some individuals have reported encountering sudden drops in temperature or feeling cold spots in specific areas of the island. These localized cold spots are often associated with paranormal activity and are believed to be indicative of the presence of spirits.

5. Physical Touch or Interactions: Several accounts mention experiences of feeling touched, pushed, or having their clothing tugged by unseen hands. These physical interactions can be particularly unnerving and contribute to a feeling of being in the presence of a supernatural force.

6. Electrical Disturbances: Reports include incidents of electronic devices malfunctioning or batteries draining rapidly despite being fully charged. Such disturbances are often linked to paranormal encounters and have been reported in haunted locations worldwide.

7. Emotional Resonance: Visitors have reported experiencing strong emotions, such as sadness, despair, or anger, while on Poveglia Island. These emotional responses are believed to be influenced by the tragic history of the location and the residual energy left behind by past events.

8. Lost Time or Disorientation: Some accounts mention feelings of losing track of time or experiencing disorientation while exploring the island. These sensations can be associated with encounters in locations believed to be haunted.

9. Shared Experiences: Multiple visitors have independently reported similar phenomena, such as hearing the same voices or witnessing the same apparitions. Shared experiences among different individuals add credibility to the reported encounters.

It is important to note that these reported phenomena are subjective and may be influenced by psychological factors, environmental conditions, or cultural beliefs. While they contribute to the island's haunting reputation, they remain speculative and cannot be scientifically validated. Paranormal experiences are highly personal and subjective, and interpretations of such encounters can vary significantly among individuals.

42

Chapter 6: Haunting Tales and Urban Legends

Poveglia Island's haunting history has given rise to numerous ghost stories and urban legends that have been passed down through generations. These tales have evolved over time, and while their origins may vary, they all contribute to the island's chilling reputation as one of Italy's most haunted destinations. Here is a compiled list of popular ghost stories and urban legends associated with Poveglia Island:

1. The Plague Doctor's Spirit:

One of the most enduring legends involves the ghost of a plague doctor who is said to roam the abandoned buildings on Poveglia. Dressed in a dark cloak and wearing the iconic beak-like mask, the ghostly figure is believed to be the embodiment of the island's tragic history during the bubonic plague outbreaks. It is said that if anyone encounters the plague doctor's spirit, they are doomed to suffer a similar fate as the plague victims of the past.

2. The Cries of Tormented Souls:

Legend has it that the tormented souls of those who perished on Poveglia Island continue to linger, and their cries and moans can still be heard during the night. Visitors have reported eerie sounds emanating from the abandoned hospital rooms and hallways, adding to the island's haunted reputation.

3. The Lady in White:

A common ghostly apparition reported on Poveglia Island is that of a lady in white. Described as a melancholic figure clad in a flowing white gown, she is said to wander the grounds, perhaps mourning the loss of loved ones or seeking peace for her restless soul. The origin of this tale is unclear, but similar apparitions are often found in ghost lore across various cultures.

4. The Lazzaretto's Dark Secrets:

Urban legends surrounding the old Lazzaretto hospital abound, with stories of unethical medical experiments and cruel treatments inflicted upon the mentally ill patients. Tales of lobotomies, electroshock therapy, and other inhumane practices contribute to the island's sinister aura and its association with unspeakable horrors.

5. The Island's Haunted Soil:

According to some legends, the soil of Poveglia Island is cursed due to the countless plague victims and mentally ill patients buried there. It is believed that anyone who carries even a small amount of the island's soil will be plagued by bad luck and misfortune.

6. The Haunted Bell Tower:

The bell tower that stands on Poveglia Island is said to be a focal point of paranormal activity. Legend has it that the bell tolls on its own, and visitors have reported hearing its eerie chimes in the dead of night, even though the tower is no longer functional.

7. The Haunting of Poveglia's Waterways:

Legend speaks of ghostly apparitions emerging from the waters surrounding Poveglia Island. These spirits are believed to be the souls of plague victims who were cast into the lagoon, still seeking redemption or eternal rest.

8. The Lost Souls of the Mental Hospital:

Urban legends often depict the abandoned mental hospital as a hotbed of paranormal activity. Visitors claim to have seen shadowy figures moving within the buildings or heard disembodied voices whispering in the darkness, suggesting that the spirits of mentally ill patients still wander the asylum's halls.

As with most ghost stories and urban legends, the variations and details of these tales may differ depending on who tells them and how they evolve over time. Nevertheless, the collective effect of these stories has contributed to the island's enduring reputation as a place shrouded in mystery and terror.

The enduring appeal of haunting tales associated with Poveglia Island can be attributed to a combination of cultural and psychological factors. These factors play a significant role in shaping people's fascination with ghost stories and urban legends, especially those connected to places with dark and mysterious histories like Poveglia. Here's an analysis of these contributing factors:

Cultural Factors:

1. HISTORICAL SIGNIFICANCE: Poveglia Island's historical significance as a quarantine site during the bubonic plague and later as a mental hospital has laid the groundwork for its haunting reputation. Historical events involving tragedy, death, and suffering often become fertile ground for ghost stories and legends.

2. Cultural Beliefs in the Supernatural: Italy, like many other cultures, has a rich tradition of folklore and belief in the supernatural. Cultural narratives about ghosts, spirits, and haunted places have been passed down through generations, shaping people's perceptions and interpretations of mysterious phenomena.

3. Oral Tradition and Storytelling: The power of oral tradition plays a role in keeping these haunting tales alive. Stories about Poveglia Island have likely been shared among locals and visitors for years, leading to their perpetuation and adaptation over time.

4. Tourism and Dark Tourism: The allure of dark tourism, where visitors seek out places associated with death, tragedy, or the supernatural, contributes to the fascination with Poveglia Island. Haunting tales heighten the appeal of such destinations for thrill-seekers and those intrigued by the macabre.

Psychological Factors:

1. FEAR AND THRILL-Seeking: Humans have an innate fascination with fear, which can be thrilling in a controlled and safe environment. Haunting tales of Poveglia Island offer a vicarious experience of fear and adrenaline, allowing individuals to indulge in a sense of excitement and uncertainty.

2. Mystery and the Unknown: The island's off-limits status and restricted access contribute to the air of mystery surrounding Poveglia. The allure of the unknown and the forbidden spark curiosity and imagination, making the island an intriguing subject for ghost stories and urban legends.

3. Emotional Resonance: Tales of suffering, tragedy, and restless spirits evoke strong emotional responses in individuals. People might feel a sense of empathy or sadness for the alleged souls trapped on Poveglia Island, which enhances the emotional impact of the stories.

4. Confirmation Bias: For individuals who visit Poveglia Island seeking paranormal experiences, confirmation bias can come into play. People may interpret ambiguous stimuli or unusual occurrences as evidence of supernatural activity, reinforcing their belief in the haunting tales.

5. Sense of Connection to History: Haunting tales rooted in historical events create a sense of connection to the past. People might view themselves as part of a larger narrative, linking the present to the island's dark history and preserving its memory through storytelling.

The enduring appeal of haunting tales associated with Poveglia Island is influenced by a complex interplay of cultural factors and psychological motivations. The island's historical significance, cultural beliefs in the supernatural, and the allure of dark tourism contribute to its haunting reputation. On a psychological level, fear and thrill-seeking, the mystery of the unknown, emotional resonance, and confirmation bias play roles in drawing people to these tales and keeping them alive over time. The combination of these factors contributes to the enduring fascination with Poveglia's haunting history, perpetuating its reputation as a place of terror and intrigue.

POVEGLIA ISLAND: HAUNTING SECRETS OF ITALY'S MOST TERRIFYING HAUNTED DESTINATION

Chapter 7: Paranormal Investigations

Poveglia Island's chilling history and haunting reputation have drawn the attention of paranormal investigators eager to delve into the island's dark past and uncover any potential supernatural activity. These brave investigators embark on daring expeditions to explore the isolated and off-limits island, armed with a range of methodologies and specialized equipment to document their findings.

Methodologies:

1. HISTORICAL RESEARCH: Before setting foot on Poveglia Island, paranormal investigators begin their investigations with thorough historical research. They study the island's past, including its role as a plague quarantine site and the operation of the mental hospital. Understanding the historical context provides insights into potential sources of paranormal activity and guides their exploration.

2. Ghost-Hunting Equipment: Paranormal investigators employ various sophisticated tools and equipment to detect and record potential paranormal phenomena. These may include electromagnetic field (EMF) detectors to identify fluctuations in electromagnetic energy, digital voice recorders to capture Electronic Voice Phenomena (EVPs), and thermal imaging cameras to detect temperature changes.

3. Psychic Mediums and Sensitives: Some investigators collaborate with psychic mediums or sensitives who claim to have the ability to perceive or communicate with spirits. These individuals are believed to be more attuned to the supernatural and can offer insights or guidance during the investigation.

4. Nighttime Investigations: Many paranormal investigators conduct their explorations during the nighttime, as it is believed that supernatural activity is more prevalent after dark. The eerie atmosphere of Poveglia Island's abandoned structures heightens the sense of mystery and provides an ideal setting for their investigations.

Findings:

1. EVP RECORDINGS: Several paranormal investigators claim to have captured mysterious EVP recordings during their explorations on Poveglia Island. These recordings often include unexplained voices or whispers that were not audible at the time of the investigation.

2. Temperature Fluctuations: Investigators have reported sudden drops in temperature, often referred to as "cold spots," which are commonly associated with paranormal activity. These fluctuations occur in specific areas and cannot be attributed to environmental factors.

3. Unexplained EMF Readings: EMF detectors have registered anomalous electromagnetic fluctuations in certain locations on the island. These readings are believed to be indicative of the presence of spirits or paranormal energy.

4. Apparitions and Shadow Figures: Some investigators claim to have witnessed shadowy figures or apparitions moving through the abandoned buildings. These ghostly forms are often fleeting and elusive, adding to the chilling atmosphere of the island.

5. Personal Experiences: Many investigators share personal experiences, such as feeling touched or hearing unexplained noises while exploring Poveglia. These encounters contribute to their belief in the island's haunted reputation.

6. Confirmation of Legends: The investigations sometimes provide evidence that corroborates the island's haunting tales and urban legends. For example, EVP recordings may match the descriptions of the Lady in White or the cries of tormented souls.

It is essential to note that paranormal investigations and their findings are highly subjective and open to interpretation. Skeptics often attribute the reported phenomena to environmental factors, psychological influences, or misinterpretation of data. Nevertheless, paranormal investigators continue to be drawn to Poveglia Island, seeking to unravel its mysteries and document any potential evidence of the supernatural, contributing to the enduring fascination with the island's haunting history.

The scientific rigor of paranormal investigations exploring Poveglia Island's alleged supernatural phenomena faces several challenges and potential flaws. While paranormal investigators strive to approach their work with professionalism and objectivity, the nature of studying the supernatural introduces inherent biases and limitations. Here is an evaluation of the scientific rigor and potential flaws in these investigations:

Scientific Rigor:

1. USE OF SPECIALIZED Equipment: Paranormal investigators employ various specialized tools and equipment to capture data during their investigations. Devices like EMF detectors, thermal cameras, and digital voice recorders are essential for data collection, and their use demonstrates a level of methodological rigor.

2. Data Documentation: Investigators often meticulously document their findings, including the location, date, and time of each encounter or recorded phenomena. This documentation allows for a systematic analysis of the data and aids in identifying patterns or correlations.

3. Historical Research: Initiating investigations with historical research shows a commitment to understanding the context of the alleged hauntings. This background information helps investigators identify potential sources of paranormal activity and approach the investigation with informed perspectives.

4. Open-Mindedness: The best paranormal investigators approach their work with open-mindedness, considering multiple possibilities for any observed phenomena and avoiding preconceived conclusions.

Potential Flaws and Biases:

1. CONFIRMATION BIAS: Investigators and participants may experience confirmation bias, wherein they interpret ambiguous data or experiences in a way that supports their preexisting beliefs in the supernatural. This bias could lead to the misinterpretation of ordinary environmental factors as paranormal phenomena.

2. Subjectivity and Interpretation: Paranormal phenomena are by nature subjective and difficult to quantify. Interpretation of data, especially involving EVP recordings or unexplained EMF fluctuations, can vary widely among investigators.

3. Lack of Control Group: Proper scientific investigations require the inclusion of control groups to distinguish between natural and supernatural explanations. However, paranormal investigations often lack control groups due to the unpredictable nature of the phenomena being studied.

4. Environmental Factors: Environmental factors, such as temperature changes, drafts, or faulty equipment, can influence the data collected during investigations. Differentiating between genuine paranormal occurrences and ordinary environmental events is challenging.

5. Psychological Influences: Human perception can be influenced by psychological factors, leading to the misinterpretation of experiences or the exaggeration of sensations during investigations.

6. Lack of Reproducibility: One of the cornerstones of scientific rigor is the ability to reproduce findings independently. However, the sporadic and unpredictable nature of paranormal phenomena makes it challenging to replicate investigations consistently.

In summary, while paranormal investigations exploring Poveglia Island's haunting tales strive to adhere to scientific methods, they face inherent limitations and potential biases. The subjectivity of paranormal experiences, the lack of control groups, and the influence of confirmation bias all contribute to the challenges in maintaining scientific rigor in these investigations. Consequently, the findings of such studies are often regarded skeptically by the broader scientific community, who advocate for more controlled and reproducible methods in the study of supernatural phenomena.

POVEGLIA ISLAND: HAUNTING SECRETS OF ITALY'S MOST TERRIFYING HAUNTED DESTINATION

Chapter 8: Supernatural Evidence

Analyzing photographic and video evidence claimed to capture paranormal activity on Poveglia Island requires a critical and impartial examination. It is important to approach such evidence with skepticism and apply scientific scrutiny to determine its validity. Here are the key aspects to consider when evaluating photographic and video evidence of alleged paranormal activity:

1. Source and Authenticity:

The first step in analyzing paranormal evidence is to verify its source and authenticity. Investigate the individuals or teams who captured the footage to assess their credibility and expertise in paranormal investigations. Look for any signs of tampering or manipulation that could raise doubts about the evidence's authenticity.

2. Context and Conditions:

Consider the context in which the evidence was collected. Assess the environmental conditions, such as lighting, weather, and time of day, as they can impact the quality and interpretation of the footage. Unusual lighting or camera glitches might lead to artifacts that appear as paranormal activity but have rational explanations.

3. Corroborating Testimony:

Evaluate any testimonies provided by the investigators or witnesses who captured the evidence. Multiple accounts of the same paranormal activity can lend credibility to the claims, but inconsistencies among witness statements could raise concerns about the reliability of the evidence.

4. Explanations for Anomalies:

Before attributing anomalies in the footage to paranormal activity, explore mundane explanations. Reflect on possible natural phenomena, camera malfunctions, or artifacts caused by reflections, shadows, or dust particles. Often, ordinary occurrences can appear strange in photographs or videos.

5. Comparative Analysis:

Compare the alleged paranormal evidence with normal footage captured during the same investigation. By analyzing other footage from the same location and time, you can identify discrepancies that might reveal inconsistencies in the evidence.

6. Skeptical Review:

Invite the opinions of skeptical experts who can provide an unbiased evaluation of the evidence. Skeptics are valuable in scrutinizing claims from a scientific and rational standpoint, helping to eliminate biases and wishful thinking.

7. Reproducibility and Independent Verification:

Ideally, paranormal evidence should be reproducible and verifiable by independent investigators. The ability to capture the same phenomena in different circumstances strengthens the validity of the claims.

8. Critical Thinking:

Approach the analysis with critical thinking, considering alternative explanations for the phenomena depicted in the footage. Avoid drawing hasty conclusions based solely on a desire for the evidence to support paranormal activity.

Photographic and video evidence of alleged paranormal activity on Poveglia Island requires careful analysis and skepticism. Without rigorous scientific scrutiny and independent verification, such evidence remains speculative and cannot be considered definitive proof of the supernatural. While intriguing, it is essential to remain objective and open-minded while exploring the mysteries of Poveglia Island and to consider all possible explanations before attributing any anomalies to paranormal phenomena.

Examination of Evidence Authenticity:

THE AUTHENTICITY OF paranormal evidence captured on Poveglia Island is a subject of considerable debate. While proponents believe the evidence supports the existence of supernatural activity, skeptics raise doubts about its legitimacy. Here's an analysis of the evidence's authenticity:

1. Photographs:

- Proponents: Those who support the authenticity of paranormal photographs argue that the captured anomalies, such as orbs, shadow figures, or unexplained light sources, cannot be explained by ordinary environmental factors or camera glitches. They claim that these visual phenomena are consistent with ghostly apparitions or spiritual energy.

● Skeptics: Skeptics argue that many alleged paranormal photographs can be attributed to lens flares, dust particles, lens artifacts, or reflections. They emphasize the need to consider mundane explanations before assuming that such anomalies are paranormal in nature.

2. Video Recordings:

● Proponents: Believers in the authenticity of paranormal video evidence assert that it captures movements, apparitions, or unexplained disturbances in the environment that cannot be easily explained by natural occurrences. They argue that these recordings provide visual proof of supernatural activity on the island.

● Skeptics: Skeptics point out that video recordings can be prone to manipulation or misinterpretation. They caution against assuming that anomalous movements or unexplained disturbances are automatically paranormal, as they could be caused by camera movement, reflections, or environmental factors.

3. EVP Recordings:

- Proponents: Supporters of EVP recordings claim that they capture unexplained voices or messages from the spirit world. They argue that the voices are distinct from any known human or environmental sources, indicating communication from the afterlife.

- Skeptics: Skeptics suggest that EVP recordings may be influenced by various factors, such as background noise, pareidolia (perceiving patterns in random data), or audio matrixing (interpreting random sounds as meaningful speech). They propose that the claimed messages could be unintentional artifacts of audio manipulation.

Arguments Presented by Skeptics and Believers:

1. SKEPTICS' ARGUMENTS:

- Scientific Rigor: Skeptics advocate for rigorous scientific methodologies and controlled experiments to substantiate claims of paranormal activity. They criticize the lack of standardization and objectivity in many paranormal investigations.

- Logical Fallacies: Skeptics point out logical fallacies in believers' arguments, such as the appeal to emotion or the argument from ignorance (assuming something is true simply because it cannot be disproven).

● Reproducibility: Skeptics emphasize the importance of reproducibility in paranormal research. They argue that isolated instances of alleged activity do not constitute evidence without consistent results in different settings.

2. Believers' Arguments:

● Personal Experience: Believers often cite their own personal experiences as strong evidence for the existence of paranormal activity. They argue that firsthand encounters with unexplained phenomena are compelling proof of the supernatural.

● Anecdotal Evidence: Believers present anecdotal accounts from witnesses who claim to have encountered paranormal occurrences on Poveglia Island. They assert that the accumulation of such accounts strengthens the case for its haunted reputation.

● Existence of the Unexplained: Believers argue that some evidence remains unexplained despite skeptical analyses. They contend that while not all anomalies may be paranormal, there are instances that defy conventional explanations.

POVEGLIA ISLAND: HAUNTING SECRETS OF ITALY'S MOST TERRIFYING HAUNTED DESTINATION

The authenticity of paranormal evidence from Poveglia Island remains a subject of ongoing debate between skeptics and believers. While believers find the evidence compelling and suggestive of supernatural activity, skeptics emphasize the need for scientific rigor and the consideration of mundane explanations. Ultimately, conclusive proof of the existence of the paranormal would require well-controlled and reproducible scientific investigations, which remain challenging in the realm of supernatural phenomena. As such, the debate surrounding Poveglia Island's haunting tales and the authenticity of its evidence continues to be a subject of fascination and skepticism.

Chapter 9: The Psychological Impact of Haunted Places

The psychological effects experienced by individuals who visit or spend time on allegedly haunted locations like Poveglia can be diverse and vary depending on the person's beliefs, past experiences, and the intensity of the haunting legends associated with the location. Here are some common psychological effects reported by individuals who visit such places:

1. Fear and Anxiety: One of the most immediate and common psychological responses to allegedly haunted locations is fear and anxiety. The eerie atmosphere, dark history, and haunted tales of Poveglia can trigger a primal fear response in visitors, especially in those who believe in ghosts or supernatural entities.

2. Heightened Sensitivity: People visiting haunted locations may report heightened sensitivity to their surroundings. They may become more attuned to sounds, shadows, and movements, attributing them to paranormal activity.

3. Sensed Presence: Some individuals may report feeling as though they are being watched or that an unseen presence is near them. This phenomenon, known as the "sensed presence," can contribute to feelings of unease and fear.

4. Vivid Imaginations and Hallucinations: The haunted reputation of Poveglia Island can fuel people's imaginations, leading to the perception of things that may not be present. In dimly lit or unsettling environments, individuals may experience hallucinations or misinterpret natural occurrences as paranormal activity.

5. Emotional Responses: Haunted locations like Poveglia, with their tragic histories, can evoke strong emotional responses in visitors. They may experience sadness, grief, or a sense of heaviness, possibly related to the historical suffering and death associated with the place.

6. Intrusive Thoughts and Obsessions: After visiting allegedly haunted locations, some individuals may develop intrusive thoughts or obsessions related to their experience. They may continuously think about the visit or have recurring thoughts of the paranormal phenomena they believe they encountered.

7. Post-Visit Rumination: The impact of visiting haunted locations may extend beyond the visit itself. People may ruminate on their experiences, discussing and replaying them with others or in their minds, which can further heighten their psychological effects.

8. Confirmation Bias: Individuals who strongly believe in the paranormal may interpret ambiguous or normal occurrences as evidence of ghosts or supernatural activity. This confirmation bias can reinforce their preexisting beliefs and contribute to a lasting conviction of the location's haunted nature.

9. Positive Emotions and Thrill-Seeking: Not all psychological effects are negative. Some individuals may experience positive emotions and thrill-seeking excitement from visiting allegedly haunted locations. The adrenaline rush and excitement of exploring eerie environments can be enjoyable for some people.

It's important to note that the psychological effects experienced by individuals at haunted locations are subjective and can vary widely. People with a history of anxiety, trauma, or preexisting beliefs in the supernatural may be more susceptible to intense psychological responses. The power of suggestion, group dynamics, and the overall social context of the visit can also influence how individuals perceive and respond to allegedly haunted locations like Poveglia Island.

The power of suggestion and belief plays a significant role in shaping the experiences of individuals who visit allegedly haunted locations like Poveglia Island. Psychologists and experts have explored these phenomena through various studies and research.

The placebo effect is a well-documented psychological phenomenon where a person's belief in the effectiveness of a treatment or intervention can lead to real physiological or psychological changes. Similarly, the expectation bias, also known as the "experimenter effect," occurs when individuals unconsciously conform their behavior or perceptions to match what they believe is expected of them.

In the context of haunted locations, visitors who firmly believe in ghosts or paranormal activity are more likely to experience or interpret ambiguous stimuli as paranormal phenomena. Their heightened expectations create a feedback loop, reinforcing their beliefs and leading to a higher likelihood of reporting paranormal experiences.

The power of suggestion can be magnified in group settings, particularly during visits to allegedly haunted locations. Social influence and group dynamics can foster a collective belief in the supernatural, leading individuals to experience and interpret similar phenomena in a way that aligns with the group narrative.

In such settings, individuals may be more likely to conform to the group's beliefs, amplifying the impact of the suggestion and increasing the likelihood of shared paranormal experiences. This phenomenon can be seen in ghost tours, paranormal investigations, or when friends visit haunted locations together.

Emotional contagion refers to the phenomenon of one person's emotions and related behaviors spreading to others within a group. In haunted locations, if one individual becomes fearful or anxious due to the belief in ghosts or the haunting history of the place, others in the group may also experience similar emotions, even if they initially had no such feelings.

Shared emotional experiences can lead to collective feelings of fear or excitement, reinforcing the belief in the paranormal and intensifying the overall experience of the haunted location.

POVEGLIA ISLAND: HAUNTING SECRETS OF ITALY'S MOST TERRIFYING HAUNTED DESTINATION

Memory is reconstructive, and people often fill in gaps in their recollection based on their beliefs and expectations. After visiting a haunted location, individuals may selectively remember or emphasize the elements that align with their preexisting beliefs about ghosts or paranormal activity.

Memory biases can lead to the creation of false memories, where individuals may genuinely believe they experienced something supernatural even if it did not occur as they remember it.

Cognitive dissonance occurs when individuals hold conflicting beliefs or attitudes, leading to psychological discomfort. When confronted with experiences that challenge their beliefs about the paranormal, individuals may rationalize or justify the discrepancy to reduce cognitive dissonance.

This may manifest as a dismissal of contradictory evidence or the reinterpretation of non-paranormal events as signs of the supernatural, further reinforcing their initial beliefs.

The power of suggestion and belief significantly influences the experiences of individuals who visit allegedly haunted locations. Psychologists and experts emphasize the role of expectation bias, social influence, emotional contagion, memory biases, and cognitive dissonance in shaping these experiences. Understanding these psychological mechanisms provides valuable insights into how individuals interpret and respond to the haunting legends and paranormal stories associated with places like Poveglia Island.

Chapter 10: The Island's Influence on Popular Culture

Poveglia Island's haunting reputation has made it a subject of fascination in various forms of artistic expression. Here are some key instances where Poveglia Island has been referenced in movies, literature, music, and art:

Movies:

1. "ISLE OF THE DEAD" (1945): This horror film directed by Mark Robson takes place on a fictional Greek island but draws inspiration from the legends and stories surrounding Poveglia Island. It explores themes of isolation, death, and the fear of contagion.

2. "The Plague" (2006): Directed by Hal Masonberg, this horror film features a fictional island where a deadly plague breaks out. The island's quarantine measures are reminiscent of Poveglia's history as a plague quarantine site.

3. "The Asylum" (2015): This found footage horror film revolves around a group of paranormal investigators who visit a haunted asylum, and it draws inspiration from the legends of Poveglia's mental hospital.

Literature:

1. "THE LITTLE BOOK of True Ghost Stories" (2001): This collection by Echo Bodine includes a chapter on Poveglia Island, recounting its history and haunted reputation.

2. "Ghost Island" (2018): Written by Charles Benoit, this young adult novel features a fictional island called "Ghost Island," inspired by the legends of Poveglia.

Music:

1. "POVEGLIA" BY ABORTED (2012): This song by the death metal band Aborted references Poveglia Island in its lyrics, capturing the theme of morbidity and death associated with the location.

2. "Poveglia" by Stillborn (2016): Another song titled "Poveglia," by the death metal band Stillborn, explores the dark history and haunted legends of the island.

Art:

1. "POVEGLIA" BY CARL Dobsky: This haunting digital painting depicts a dark, eerie scene on Poveglia Island, capturing the sense of desolation and dread associated with the location.

2. "Poveglia Island Series" by Jave Yoshimoto: This series of mixed media artworks explores the haunting history of Poveglia Island and its connection to themes of mortality and the supernatural.

POVEGLIA ISLAND: HAUNTING SECRETS OF ITALY'S MOST TERRIFYING HAUNTED DESTINATION

These instances demonstrate how Poveglia Island has inspired artists across different mediums, utilizing its chilling history and haunting tales to create works that evoke a sense of mystery, fear, and fascination. The island's dark reputation as one of Italy's most haunted destinations continues to resonate in various forms of artistic expression.

The representations of Poveglia Island in movies, literature, music, and art have played a significant role in enhancing and perpetuating its reputation as a haunted location. These creative expressions leverage the island's chilling history and legends to evoke fear, curiosity, and a sense of the supernatural. Here's how these representations have contributed to the island's haunted reputation:

1. Amplifying the Legends:

Artistic representations often amplify the haunting legends associated with Poveglia Island. Movies, literature, and music tend to exaggerate the paranormal elements, depicting ghostly apparitions, eerie sounds, and malevolent spirits. These portrayals heighten the island's mystique, making it a subject of intrigue for those interested in the supernatural.

2. Spreading Cultural Awareness:

Artistic works can reach a wide audience, spreading cultural awareness about Poveglia Island's dark history and haunted tales. Through movies, novels, and songs, people from various parts of the world become familiar with the island's name and reputation as a haunted destination, further solidifying its position in popular culture.

3. Emotional Connection:

Art has the power to evoke strong emotions and connect with the audience on a personal level. By tapping into primal fears and the fear of the unknown, these representations create an emotional connection with viewers, readers, or listeners. This emotional resonance can make Poveglia Island's haunting tales more memorable and impactful, leading to lasting impressions and discussions about the island's reputation.

4. Reinforcing Beliefs and Myths:

Artistic representations often reinforce existing beliefs and myths about the supernatural. For those who already believe in ghosts or paranormal activity, these depictions validate their beliefs and provide a sense of confirmation. This validation can reinforce the island's reputation as a haunted location in the minds of believers.

5. Curiosity and Thrill-Seeking:

Poveglia Island's portrayal in artistic works sparks curiosity and thrill-seeking behavior among audiences. People who enjoy horror movies or eerie tales are drawn to stories centered around haunted locations like Poveglia. As a result, the island becomes a popular topic of discussion and exploration among those seeking a thrilling experience.

6. Influence on Tourism and Popularity:

The portrayal of Poveglia Island in artistic works has the potential to impact tourism. Haunted tourism or "dark tourism" is a growing trend, and works that depict Poveglia as a haunted destination can attract visitors eager to explore its chilling past and experience the thrill of the supernatural.

7. Perpetuation of Urban Legends:

Artistic representations can contribute to the perpetuation of urban legends surrounding Poveglia Island. As these representations are shared and disseminated through various media, they become part of the island's collective folklore, further strengthening its reputation as a place of eerie mysteries.

The representations of Poveglia Island in movies, literature, music, and art have been instrumental in shaping and reinforcing its reputation as a haunted location. Through emotional connections, spreading cultural awareness, and reinforcing existing beliefs, these creative expressions have firmly established the island's haunting tales in popular culture, making it an enduring subject of fascination and intrigue for those drawn to the supernatural and the macabre.

Chapter 11: Poveglia's Haunting Artifacts

Based on historical information, some artifacts and relics associated with Poveglia Island's past as a quarantine site and mental hospital may include:

1. Medical Equipment: Old medical instruments and equipment used during the island's time as a quarantine station and mental hospital, such as surgical tools, medical charts, and laboratory equipment.

2. Patient Records: Historical patient records, including medical files, treatment logs, and admissions records that provide insights into the individuals who were quarantined or treated on the island.

3. Personal Belongings: Personal items left behind by patients, staff, or visitors, such as clothing, shoes, personal effects, and belongings, which can give a glimpse into the lives of those who lived or worked on the island.

4. Asylum Furniture: Furniture from the former mental hospital, including beds, chairs, and tables, which may be preserved as relics of the island's past.

5. Religious Artifacts: Religious items or symbols used during the island's time as a quarantine station, such as crosses or religious icons believed to provide protection from illness.

6. Structural Remnants: Remnants of the island's buildings, including walls, doorways, and architectural features, that offer tangible evidence of its historical use.

7. Archival Documents: Historical documents, photographs, and maps related to the island's quarantine and mental hospital periods, which can provide a deeper understanding of its history.

It's essential to note that Poveglia Island has been off-limits to the public for many years, and access to artifacts and relics on the island is strictly controlled. Many historical items might be protected or housed in museums or archives for preservation. Any exploration or documentation of artifacts should be done with sensitivity and respect for the site's historical significance. If you are interested in learning more about specific artifacts or relics from Poveglia Island, I recommend reaching out to historical archives or official organizations responsible for the island's preservation and historical records.

Displaying artifacts from Poveglia Island in museums raises various ethical considerations, particularly given the island's dark history as a quarantine site and mental hospital. Additionally, the potential spiritual implications of showcasing these artifacts must be carefully examined. Here are some key ethical concerns and spiritual considerations:

1. Respect for the Deceased and Their Descendants:

Displaying artifacts from Poveglia Island should be approached with respect and sensitivity to the memory of those who suffered or died on the island. It is essential to consider the feelings and rights of their descendants, as these artifacts may hold deep personal and emotional significance for them.

2. Privacy and Dignity of Past Patients:

Many of the artifacts may have once belonged to patients of the mental hospital. Ensuring the privacy and dignity of these individuals, even in death, is crucial. Exhibiting personal items must be done in a way that honors their lives and respects their privacy.

3. Avoiding Sensationalization and Exploitation:

Museums must be cautious not to exploit the tragic history of Poveglia Island for commercial gain or sensationalism. The exhibition of artifacts should aim to educate and inform rather than capitalize on macabre or sensational aspects.

4. Informed Consent and Repatriation:

If displaying human remains or sacred objects, museums should obtain informed consent from the relevant communities or descendants. In some cases, repatriation of certain artifacts to their places of origin may be necessary, especially if they have significant spiritual or cultural value to those communities.

5. Mental Health Considerations:

Given the island's history as a mental hospital, displaying artifacts related to mental illness raises mental health considerations. Museums should take care not to perpetuate stereotypes or stigmatize individuals with mental health conditions.

6. Balancing Preservation and Respect:

Preserving historical artifacts is essential for understanding the past, but it should be balanced with respect for the people and events they represent. This balance requires careful curation and contextualization to avoid glorifying or trivializing the island's tragic history.

Spiritual Implications:

THE SPIRITUAL IMPLICATIONS of displaying artifacts from Poveglia Island are complex and may vary based on different beliefs and cultural contexts:

1. Haunted or Cursed Beliefs: Some people may believe that the artifacts from a place with a dark history like Poveglia carry negative energy or are cursed. Exhibiting such objects may be perceived as inviting spiritual disturbances or negative energies into the museum space.

2. Sacred Items: Certain artifacts may hold sacred or ritualistic significance for specific communities or religious groups. Displaying these items in a museum may raise questions of whether it is appropriate to showcase spiritual objects outside their original context.

3. Symbolic Representation: Some artifacts may symbolize the suffering and resilience of those who lived and died on the

island. Their display can serve as a reminder of historical injustices and promote empathy and understanding.

4. Spiritual Healing: For some visitors, seeing these artifacts in a museum setting may offer a form of spiritual closure or healing. Engaging with the history of the island and acknowledging past traumas may facilitate a sense of catharsis or remembrance.

Displaying artifacts from Poveglia Island in museums requires careful consideration of ethical concerns, respect for the deceased and their descendants, and awareness of potential spiritual implications. Museums should approach such exhibitions with sensitivity, cultural competence, and a commitment to educating visitors about the island's history while recognizing the dignity and humanity of those who were impacted by its past.

Chapter 12: Controversies and Skepticism

Skeptics challenge the paranormal claims associated with Poveglia Island based on rational and scientific perspectives. They approach the legends and haunting tales with a critical mindset and offer various arguments against the existence of supernatural phenomena. Here are some common arguments put forth by skeptics:

1. Lack of Empirical Evidence:

Skeptics argue that the paranormal claims regarding Poveglia Island lack empirical evidence. Extraordinary claims, such as ghost sightings or interactions with spirits, require substantial evidence to be taken seriously by the scientific community. Without verifiable data and controlled experiments, these claims remain speculative and unproven.

2. Misinterpretation of Natural Events:

Many alleged paranormal experiences on Poveglia Island can be attributed to misinterpretation of natural events. For example, flickering lights, strange sounds, or feelings of being watched can often be explained by ordinary environmental factors, such as drafts, creaking wood, or psychological influences like the power of suggestion.

3. Psychological Factors:

Skeptics point out that human perception and cognition can be influenced by psychological factors, leading individuals to interpret ordinary occurrences as paranormal events. The power of suggestion, confirmation bias, and the desire to experience something supernatural can shape people's perceptions during visits to allegedly haunted locations.

4. Urban Legends and Storytelling:

Poveglia Island's haunting reputation has been fueled by urban legends, folklore, and storytelling over the years. Skeptics argue that these stories, while intriguing, lack concrete evidence and are often embellished over time, leading to a distorted version of historical events.

5. Emotional and Social Influences:

Visiting a location with a reputation for being haunted can evoke strong emotions and create a sense of thrill and excitement. Skeptics suggest that the emotional and social aspects of such experiences can influence how individuals perceive and interpret their encounters, leading to a bias toward believing in the supernatural.

6. Inconsistent Reports:

Skeptics note that the reports of paranormal activity on Poveglia Island are often inconsistent and subjective. Different individuals may report vastly different experiences during their visits, and there is a lack of consistency in the types of phenomena reported, which raises questions about the reliability of the claims.

7. Explanations Rooted in Science:

Skeptics propose that many paranormal claims can be explained by known scientific principles, such as infrasound (low-frequency sound waves that can induce feelings of fear or unease) or the ideomotor effect (where unconscious movements lead to the perception of external forces). Exploring these scientific explanations provides more plausible interpretations for alleged supernatural events.

In summary, skeptics challenge the paranormal claims associated with Poveglia Island by advocating for empirical evidence, pointing out misinterpretation of natural events, considering psychological influences, and questioning the reliability of inconsistent reports. They emphasize the need for scientific rigor and critical thinking in exploring claims of the supernatural, including those linked to allegedly haunted locations like Poveglia Island.

Addressing common counterarguments between skeptics and believers regarding the paranormal claims associated with Poveglia Island can provide a balanced assessment of their credibility. Let's examine some common counterarguments from both sides:

1. Counterargument: Lack of Empirical Evidence (Skeptics):

Skeptics argue that the absence of concrete, scientifically verifiable evidence weakens the credibility of paranormal claims. They emphasize the need for rigorous investigations and controlled experiments to support the existence of supernatural phenomena on Poveglia Island.

Assessment: The lack of empirical evidence does present a challenge to the credibility of paranormal claims. Without reliable data and reproducible experiments, it becomes difficult to establish the validity of these claims based on scientific principles.

2. Counterargument: Personal Experiences and Testimonies (Believers):

Believers often cite their personal experiences and testimonies as strong evidence of paranormal activity on Poveglia Island. They assert that the sheer number of reported encounters cannot be ignored and should be taken seriously.

Assessment: Personal experiences and testimonies hold subjective value for individuals who have encountered allegedly paranormal phenomena. While these accounts can be compelling on an individual level, they may not meet the criteria for scientific evidence, as they lack objectivity and controlled conditions.

3. Counterargument: Skeptical Explanations (Skeptics):

Skeptics offer plausible alternative explanations for paranormal encounters on Poveglia Island, such as psychological factors, misinterpretation of natural events, and the power of suggestion. They argue that these explanations provide more rational and scientific interpretations for the reported phenomena.

Assessment: Skeptical explanations highlight the importance of considering mundane and natural causes before attributing events to the supernatural. These explanations align with established scientific principles and offer a critical perspective.

4. Counterargument: Emotional and Social Influences (Believers):

Believers argue that the emotional and social influences during visits to allegedly haunted locations are genuine responses to the paranormal. They assert that the fear and excitement experienced by visitors are authentic reactions to supernatural encounters.

Assessment: Emotional and social influences can indeed influence individuals' experiences, and it is essential to acknowledge the genuine feelings and emotions of visitors. However, emotional responses do not, in themselves, serve as empirical evidence for the existence of paranormal phenomena.

5. Counterargument: Historical Legends and Folklore (Both Sides):

Both skeptics and believers acknowledge the historical legends and folklore surrounding Poveglia Island. While skeptics view these stories as potentially exaggerating events over time, believers see them as a part of the island's haunting identity.

Assessment: Historical legends and folklore contribute to the island's reputation and cultural significance, but they do not provide direct evidence for or against the paranormal claims. These stories can be compelling and add to the intrigue, but they require critical analysis to separate fact from fiction.

The debate between skeptics and believers regarding the paranormal claims associated with Poveglia Island is characterized by contrasting perspectives on empirical evidence, personal experiences, skeptical explanations, emotional influences, and historical legends. While believers find personal experiences and historical tales compelling, skeptics emphasize the importance of empirical evidence and rational explanations rooted in scientific principles.

Assessing the credibility of both sides requires recognizing the subjective nature of personal experiences and testimonies while also acknowledging the need for objective and scientifically rigorous investigations. Ultimately, the existence of paranormal phenomena on Poveglia Island remains a subject of fascination and ongoing debate, with no definitive resolution yet reached.

POVEGLIA ISLAND: HAUNTING SECRETS OF ITALY'S MOST TERRIFYING HAUNTED DESTINATION

Chapter 13: Haunted Islands Around the World

Comparing Poveglia Island's haunting history with other infamous haunted islands around the world allows us to explore the diverse cultural factors and historical contexts that contribute to their eerie reputations. Here are some examples of other haunted islands and their unique characteristics:

1. Poveglia Island (Italy):

- Cultural Factors: Poveglia's haunting history is deeply rooted in Italian culture and folklore. Its association with the bubonic plague and later as a mental hospital adds to the island's aura of suffering, death, and torment. Italian legends and stories about the island's tragic past have been passed down through generations, shaping its reputation as one of Italy's most haunted destinations.

- Historical Context: The island's history as a quarantine station for plague victims and later as a mental hospital has left a dark legacy. The suffering and death experienced by those who were confined there contribute to its chilling reputation. The abandonment of the island and restrictions on public access have further fueled the sense of mystery and fear surrounding Poveglia.

2. Hashima Island (Japan):

- Cultural Factors: Hashima Island, also known as Gunkanjima or Battleship Island, is located off the coast of Nagasaki, Japan. Its haunting history is tied to its past as a coal mining facility where forced laborers worked under harsh conditions. The island's appearance, with its dense concrete buildings and industrial ruins, has been featured in Japanese pop culture and films, adding to its mystique.

- Historical Context: Hashima Island was a bustling coal mining facility during the early 20th century. After the decline of coal mining, the island was abandoned, leaving behind a ghost town with decaying buildings and empty streets. The haunting atmosphere and tragic history have made it a popular destination for urban explorers and photographers.

3. Poveglia Island (India):

- Cultural Factors: Located in the Sunderbans region of India, this Poveglia Island shares the same name as the Italian island but has a distinct cultural context. The Sunderbans is known for its dense mangrove forests and is believed to be inhabited by spirits and supernatural beings according to local folklore. Poveglia Island is considered a haunted place due to its association with legends of malevolent entities.

- Historical Context: The specific historical context of this Poveglia Island might not be as well-documented as the Italian counterpart, but the legends and folklore surrounding the Sunderbans region contribute to its eerie reputation. The island's isolation and dense vegetation add to the sense of mystery and fear associated with it.

POVEGLIA ISLAND: HAUNTING SECRETS OF ITALY'S MOST TERRIFYING HAUNTED DESTINATION

4. The Island of Dolls (Mexico):

- Cultural Factors: Located in the canals of Xochimilco near Mexico City, the Island of Dolls (Isla de las Munecas) is famous for its hundreds of creepy dolls hanging from trees. The island's haunting history is rooted in Mexican folklore, with legends of a girl's spirit haunting the area and the dolls being used to appease her restless soul.

- Historical Context: The Island of Dolls was originally inhabited by a hermit named Don Julian Santana Barrera. He began hanging dolls on the island as a tribute to a girl he believed had drowned nearby. Over time, the island became a tourist attraction and a symbol of eerie fascination.

The haunting histories of infamous haunted islands like Poveglia Island in Italy, Hashima Island in Japan, Poveglia Island in India, and the Island of Dolls in Mexico are shaped by a combination of cultural factors and historical contexts. Local folklore, tragic pasts, eerie appearances, and a sense of abandonment contribute to the aura of mystery, fear, and fascination surrounding these islands. Each place holds a unique place in its respective culture's imagination and continues to intrigue visitors and researchers alike, drawing attention from those curious about the supernatural and the macabre.

Poveglia Island stands out among eerie locations due to its unique features, historical significance, and chilling reputation. Here are some key factors that distinguish Poveglia from other haunted islands:

1. Dual History as a Quarantine Station and Mental Hospital:

One of the most distinctive aspects of Poveglia Island is its dual history as a quarantine station for plague victims and a mental hospital. This combination of suffering and death associated with both infectious diseases and mental illness creates a multifaceted haunting history, making it a place with a layered and complex aura of tragedy.

2. Intense Haunting Legends and Local Folklore:

Poveglia Island's haunting legends and local folklore have been passed down through generations, contributing to its chilling reputation. Tales of plague victims being burned and tortured, as well as reports of inhumane treatments of mental patients, have become deeply ingrained in Italian culture. These stories add to the island's aura of mystery and fear.

3. Restricted Access and Abandonment:

Unlike some other haunted locations, Poveglia Island is off-limits to the public and has been abandoned for many years. The Italian government strictly controls access to the island due to its fragile state and concerns about preserving its historical significance. This restriction adds to the island's allure and makes it even more mysterious and intriguing for those curious about its haunting past.

4. Proximity to Venice and Its Surroundings:

Poveglia Island's proximity to the city of Venice, with its rich history and cultural significance, further enhances its uniqueness. The island's haunting tales are intertwined with the history of Venice and its surrounding areas, making it a part of Italy's historical tapestry and cultural heritage.

5. Potential Archaeological and Historical Significance:

As an island with a long history, Poveglia has the potential to hold valuable archaeological and historical evidence. Aside from the haunted legends, the island's past as a quarantine site and mental hospital could provide insights into medical practices, public health measures, and the treatment of mental illness during different time periods.

6. Popularity in Pop Culture and Paranormal Media:

Poveglia Island's haunting reputation has captured the attention of the paranormal community, leading to its inclusion in various TV shows, documentaries, and books about haunted locations. Its popularity in pop culture further distinguishes it among eerie destinations globally.

7. Haunting Architectural Remnants:

The remnants of the island's past, such as the crumbling buildings of the former mental hospital and quarantine facilities, create a haunting ambiance. These architectural relics stand as silent witnesses to the island's dark history, adding to its unique character.

Poveglia Island stands out among other eerie locations due to its dual history as a quarantine station and mental hospital, intense haunting legends and folklore, restricted access, proximity to Venice, potential archaeological significance, and its popularity in pop culture and paranormal media. These unique features make Poveglia Island a haunting destination that continues to captivate the imagination and curiosity of people interested in the supernatural and the macabre.

POVEGLIA ISLAND: HAUNTING SECRETS OF ITALY'S MOST TERRIFYING HAUNTED DESTINATION

Chapter 14: The Future of Poveglia

Conservationists and heritage experts recognize the historical significance of Poveglia Island and are committed to preserving its haunting past and protecting it from deterioration. Their plans focus on a combination of restoration efforts, documentation, and responsible management to ensure the island's cultural and historical heritage is safeguarded for future generations. Here are some key aspects of their preservation initiatives:

1. Documentation of Historical Artifacts and Structures:

Conservationists and experts conduct thorough documentation of the island's historical artifacts, buildings, and structures. This process involves detailed surveys, photography, and archival research to create comprehensive records of Poveglia's history. Such documentation ensures that valuable historical information is preserved even if physical restoration becomes challenging.

2. Restoration and Stabilization of Architectural Remnants:

Where feasible, conservationists work on the restoration and stabilization of the island's architectural remnants, such as the buildings of the former mental hospital and quarantine facilities. Specialized teams carefully assess the structural integrity and implement preservation techniques to prevent further decay and damage.

3. Implementation of Controlled Access Measures:

To protect the island from deterioration caused by unrestricted visits, conservationists advocate for controlled access measures. Limiting the number of visitors and establishing guided tours help reduce human impact on the fragile environment and historical structures.

4. Collaboration with Local Authorities and Institutions:

Conservationists collaborate with local authorities, historical institutions, and relevant organizations to garner support for preservation efforts. Engaging with the community and stakeholders fosters a shared sense of responsibility for Poveglia's heritage.

5. Raising Public Awareness and Funding:

Conservationists work to raise public awareness about Poveglia Island's historical significance and the importance of preserving its haunting past. Educational programs, exhibits, and media campaigns aim to garner public support and attract funding for conservation initiatives.

6. Promotion of Responsible Tourism:

Heritage experts advocate for responsible tourism practices on Poveglia Island. Emphasizing ethical behavior, respect for historical artifacts, and adherence to preservation guidelines ensures that tourism contributes positively to the island's preservation without causing harm.

7. Scientific Research and Archaeological Studies:

Conservationists prioritize scientific research and archaeological studies on Poveglia Island. These investigations uncover new historical insights and validate the significance of the island's past, supporting preservation efforts with evidence-based knowledge.

8. Conservation Zoning and Environmental Protection:

Creating conservation zones and implementing environmental protection measures help safeguard the island's natural habitats and prevent habitat destruction. Balancing conservation efforts with the island's ecological integrity ensures a holistic approach to preservation.

9. International Collaboration and Recognition:

Heritage experts may seek international collaboration and recognition for Poveglia Island's historical significance. Partnering with global conservation organizations and advocating for its inclusion in heritage lists can bolster preservation efforts.

Conservationists and heritage experts are dedicated to preserving Poveglia Island's historical significance and protecting it from deterioration. Through restoration, documentation, controlled access, responsible tourism, research, and international collaboration, they strive to safeguard the island's haunting past for generations to come. Their collective efforts reflect a commitment to maintaining Poveglia Island as a place of historical importance, cultural value, and chilling fascination.

Balancing preservation and public interest for Poveglia Island's future requires thoughtful planning and consideration. While the island's haunting history and delicate state make it challenging to open it to unrestricted tourism, there are potential uses that can strike a balance between preservation and public engagement. Here are some ideas for the island's future:

1. Historical and Cultural Tours:

Offering guided historical and cultural tours led by knowledgeable guides can allow visitors to learn about Poveglia Island's haunting past while adhering to preservation guidelines. These tours would ensure controlled access to sensitive areas, protecting the island's fragile structures and artifacts.

2. Educational Center and Museum:

Creating an educational center or museum on the island can serve as a hub for sharing information about its history, the bubonic plague, and the mental hospital. Interactive exhibits, artifacts, and multimedia displays can help visitors understand the island's significance and the importance of preservation.

3. Research and Archaeological Studies:

Encouraging ongoing research and archaeological studies on Poveglia Island can contribute to understanding its history and cultural heritage. These studies would be conducted with preservation in mind, respecting the island's fragile environment and historical remains.

POVEGLIA ISLAND: HAUNTING SECRETS OF ITALY'S MOST TERRIFYING HAUNTED DESTINATION

4. Artist Residencies and Creative Retreats:

Promoting artist residencies and creative retreats on Poveglia Island can attract artists, writers, and researchers interested in its haunting atmosphere. Artists can find inspiration in the island's unique setting while contributing to public awareness of its preservation needs.

5. Nature and Wildlife Conservation:

Poveglia Island's natural habitats are valuable and should be protected. Designating certain areas for nature and wildlife conservation can enhance biodiversity while providing opportunities for eco-tourism and educational programs about the island's ecological importance.

6. Events and Cultural Festivals:

Organizing occasional cultural festivals, art exhibitions, or historical events on the island can bring attention to its haunting history in a controlled manner. These events can be curated to respect preservation guidelines and align with the island's cultural heritage.

7. Virtual Reality Experiences:

For those who cannot physically visit the island, creating virtual reality experiences can offer a sense of exploration and immersion into Poveglia's haunting past. Virtual tours can be designed to provide educational and informative experiences while protecting the island from additional foot traffic.

8. Collaboration with Conservation Organizations:

Partnering with reputable conservation organizations can help fund preservation efforts and ensure that the island's haunting history remains protected. Such collaborations can bring expertise and resources to sustainably manage the island's preservation and public engagement.

9. Contemplative Spaces and Gardens:

Designing contemplative spaces and gardens on the island can provide visitors with areas to reflect on its haunting past and the importance of preservation. These spaces can encourage mindfulness while respecting the island's historical and ecological sensitivity.

The key to balancing preservation and public interest for Poveglia Island's future lies in thoughtful planning and responsible management. By offering controlled access, educational opportunities, cultural experiences, and partnerships with conservation organizations, the island can continue to intrigue and educate visitors while safeguarding its haunting history and natural beauty for generations to come.

POVEGLIA ISLAND: HAUNTING SECRETS OF ITALY'S MOST TERRIFYING HAUNTED DESTINATION

Chapter 15: The Occult and Poveglia

Over the years, Poveglia Island has become the subject of various rumors and claims of occult practices, rituals, and witchcraft. These stories add to the island's haunting reputation and have been fueled by its dark history as a quarantine site and mental hospital. While there is limited concrete evidence to support these claims, the legends and folklore surrounding Poveglia have contributed to its mystique as a place associated with supernatural forces. Here are some of the rumors and claims associated with occult practices and witchcraft on Poveglia:

1. Alleged Rituals and Occult Gatherings:

According to local legends and accounts from visitors, there have been rumors of clandestine rituals and occult gatherings taking place on Poveglia Island. Some stories suggest that individuals or groups have sought to commune with spirits or perform rituals believed to harness supernatural energies.

2. Witches and Accusations of Witchcraft:

In historical contexts, during the times of plague outbreaks and witch hunts, some individuals accused of practicing witchcraft were banished to Poveglia Island. This association with accused witches adds to the island's mystique and its potential connections to occult beliefs.

3. Supernatural Energy and Vortexes:

Some individuals claim to sense an otherworldly or supernatural energy on the island. They believe that certain areas may act as vortexes or points of concentrated spiritual energy, attracting those interested in occult practices and paranormal phenomena.

4. Pagan Beliefs and Folk Traditions:

Poveglia Island's haunting tales have become entwined with local pagan beliefs and folk traditions. These beliefs often involve reverence for natural elements, spirits of the land, and ancient rituals, leading to claims that such practices may have occurred or continue to occur on the island.

5. Charms and Talismans Left Behind:

Visitors and urban explorers have reported finding charms, talismans, and offerings left behind on the island. These objects are often associated with protective or spiritual purposes, suggesting that some individuals may believe in the island's supernatural powers.

6. New Age and Paranormal Enthusiasts:

The reputation of Poveglia Island as a haunted destination has attracted New Age and paranormal enthusiasts. Some of these individuals may engage in explorations, investigations, or personal rituals that add to the rumors and claims of occult practices on the island.

7. Amplification in Popular Culture:

POVEGLIA ISLAND: HAUNTING SECRETS OF ITALY'S MOST TERRIFYING HAUNTED DESTINATION

The portrayal of Poveglia Island in popular culture, including books, movies, and documentaries, has further amplified the rumors and claims of occult practices. Fictional portrayals of witches, dark rituals, and paranormal occurrences contribute to the island's association with the occult.

It is essential to approach these claims with a critical mindset, considering that many of the stories are based on legends, folklore, and personal experiences. While Poveglia Island's history is undeniably tragic and haunting, the connection to occult practices remains shrouded in mystery and speculation. The fascination with the supernatural and the macabre has contributed to the enduring allure of Poveglia as one of Italy's most terrifying haunted destinations.

The historical context of beliefs in occult practices, witchcraft, and supernatural phenomena on Poveglia Island is deeply intertwined with broader cultural and societal factors. Understanding the historical context sheds light on why such beliefs have persisted and contributed to the island's haunting reputation:

1. Witch Hunts and Persecution:

During the European witch hunts of the late medieval and early modern periods, accusations of witchcraft were rampant. People believed that witches made pacts with the devil and practiced dark rituals to harm others. Poveglia Island's association with the plague and its use as a quarantine site made it a place where the marginalized and accused were banished, further fueling its connection to witchcraft in local folklore.

2. Fear of the Unknown and Isolation:

Poveglia Island's isolation and its history as a quarantine site for plague victims and later as a mental hospital created an atmosphere of fear and desolation. In times of crisis and uncertainty, people often turn to supernatural explanations to make sense of their surroundings and cope with fear and loss. This fear of the unknown and the island's eerie atmosphere perpetuated the belief in supernatural forces and occult practices.

3. Cultural Beliefs and Folklore:

Italy, like many other cultures, has a rich tradition of folklore, superstitions, and beliefs in the supernatural. These cultural elements are passed down through generations, shaping the way people perceive and interpret their surroundings. Poveglia Island's haunting history became entwined with local folklore, weaving tales of dark rituals and malevolent spirits into its cultural fabric.

4. Popular Media and Urban Legends:

As the stories of Poveglia Island spread through oral tradition and local folklore, they also found their way into popular media, including books, movies, and documentaries. Fictional portrayals of witches, occult practices, and paranormal occurrences have perpetuated the island's haunting reputation, reaching a wider audience and reinforcing existing beliefs.

5. New Age and Paranormal Interest:

The rise of New Age spirituality and paranormal interest has led to an increased fascination with haunted locations and the supernatural. Poveglia Island's reputation as a terrifying haunted destination has attracted paranormal enthusiasts and urban explorers seeking to experience its eerie atmosphere and potentially encounter supernatural phenomena.

6. Dark Tourism and Thrill-Seeking:

Dark tourism, the practice of visiting places associated with death, tragedy, and the macabre, has gained popularity in recent years. Poveglia Island's haunting history makes it a prime destination for thrill-seekers and those curious about the unknown, further perpetuating its reputation as a place of occult significance.

The beliefs in occult practices, witchcraft, and supernatural phenomena on Poveglia Island are deeply rooted in historical, cultural, and societal contexts. The island's history as a quarantine station, mental hospital, and alleged place of exile for accused witches created an atmosphere of fear, isolation, and suffering.

These factors, combined with local folklore, popular media portrayals, and contemporary fascination with the paranormal, have perpetuated the haunting reputation of Poveglia as a place of eerie fascination and chilling legends. The blending of historical facts, cultural beliefs, and fictional elements has contributed to the enduring allure and mystique of Poveglia Island as one of Italy's most terrifying haunted destinations.

Chapter 16: Supernatural Tourism

The economic impact of supernatural tourism on Poveglia Island and the surrounding region can be significant, as it attracts visitors from both Italy and around the world. This unique form of tourism is driven by the island's haunting reputation and the fascination with the supernatural and the macabre. Here are some aspects of the economic impact:

1. Increased Tourist Revenue:

Supernatural tourism has led to an increase in tourist revenue for Poveglia Island and the surrounding region. Visitors who come to explore the haunting history and experience the eerie atmosphere contribute to the local economy by spending money on accommodations, food, transportation, and souvenirs.

2. Job Creation and Employment Opportunities:

The influx of tourists to the region has created job opportunities for local residents. Tourism-related businesses such as hotels, restaurants, tour guides, and souvenir shops have expanded to cater to the growing demand, providing employment and income to the local community.

3. Promotion of Local Culture and Heritage:

Supernatural tourism can also promote the local culture and heritage of the surrounding region. As visitors explore Poveglia

Island and learn about its haunting history, they may also engage in other cultural activities and experiences in nearby towns and cities, supporting local artisans and cultural initiatives.

4. Investment in Infrastructure and Services:

The increased interest in supernatural tourism has prompted investments in the improvement of infrastructure and services in the region. Local authorities and businesses may upgrade transportation facilities, historical sites, and tourism infrastructure to cater to the growing number of visitors.

5. Challenges in Preservation:

While supernatural tourism can bring economic benefits, it also poses challenges for the preservation of the island's historical significance. The increase in foot traffic and tourism-related activities can impact the fragile remains and structures on Poveglia Island, necessitating careful management and conservation efforts.

6. Balancing Sustainable Tourism and Conservation:

Preserving the haunting reputation of Poveglia Island while ensuring its sustainable tourism is a delicate balance. Striking a compromise between allowing visitors to experience the island's haunting past and safeguarding its fragile environment requires careful planning and management.

7. Dependency on Seasonal and Niche Tourism:

POVEGLIA ISLAND: HAUNTING SECRETS OF ITALY'S MOST TERRIFYING HAUNTED DESTINATION

Supernatural tourism tends to be seasonal and niche-oriented. The popularity of such tourism is often linked to Halloween or specific events related to the supernatural. As a result, the economic impact may fluctuate throughout the year and depend on the sustained interest in the paranormal.

8. Positive Branding for the Region:

The reputation of Poveglia Island as a haunted destination can have positive branding effects for the surrounding region. It can attract attention from media, tourism authorities, and travelers interested in unique and off-the-beaten-path experiences.

Supernatural tourism has had a notable economic impact on Poveglia Island and the surrounding region. The fascination with the island's haunting history and its association with the supernatural has attracted visitors and provided opportunities for economic growth and development. However, it also presents challenges in balancing tourism with preservation and ensuring the sustainability of the island's haunting reputation while safeguarding its historical significance for future generations. Effective management and responsible tourism practices are vital to harness the economic benefits while preserving the cultural heritage and natural environment of Poveglia Island.

Promoting haunted locations as tourist attractions raises several ethical implications that need careful consideration. While supernatural tourism can generate economic benefits and cultural interest, it also poses ethical challenges that should not be overlooked. Here are some of the key ethical concerns:

1. Exploitation of Tragic History:

Haunted locations are often associated with tragic events, suffering, and death. Promoting these places solely for entertainment or thrill-seeking purposes may be seen as exploiting the pain and trauma of those who endured these historical events. It raises questions about the appropriateness of commercializing such sensitive and often painful histories.

2. Respect for the Deceased:

Haunted locations are often the final resting places for those who lived and died there. Encouraging tourism that involves intrusive and disrespectful behavior, such as trespassing or disturbing graves, disregards the dignity and respect owed to the deceased.

3. Distortion of Historical Facts:

The commercial promotion of haunted locations may lead to the distortion of historical facts and perpetuation of myths and legends. This can undermine accurate historical education and present a skewed representation of the past, blurring the lines between reality and fiction.

4. Impact on Local Communities:

Intense tourism activity can disrupt the lives of local residents and communities. Haunted locations may become overrun with tourists, affecting the privacy and quality of life for those who live nearby. Additionally, tourism-focused developments might not always align with the needs and values of the local community.

5. Conservation and Preservation Challenges:

Increased visitation can strain the delicate environments and historical structures of haunted locations. Preserving the authenticity and historical significance of these places while accommodating tourism demands requires a delicate balance.

6. Exploitation of Beliefs:

Promoting haunted locations can also exploit the beliefs and fears of visitors who genuinely believe in the supernatural. Some tourists may be seeking validation for their beliefs, while others may be inadvertently misled into attributing mundane experiences to paranormal phenomena.

7. Informed Consent of Visitors:

Supernatural tourism often involves experiences that evoke fear and discomfort. Tourists should provide informed consent, knowing what to expect during their visit, and be aware of any potentially distressing or triggering elements.

8. Impacts on Spirituality and Culture:

For locations considered sacred or spiritually significant by certain cultures or communities, promoting them as haunted attractions can be seen as disrespectful and offensive. It may trivialize sacred beliefs and practices.

9. Responsible Marketing and Storytelling:

The way haunted locations are marketed and the stories told about them must be responsible and respectful. Sensationalizing tragedies and exploiting fear for promotional purposes can be ethically problematic.

Promoting haunted locations as tourist attractions entails a complex set of ethical considerations. While supernatural tourism can generate economic benefits and cultural interest, it requires responsible and respectful practices that balance historical preservation, cultural sensitivity, and the well-being of local communities. Striking this balance is crucial to ensure that the promotion of haunted locations respects the dignity of the deceased, accurately reflects historical facts, and offers an authentic and ethically sound experience for visitors.

POVEGLIA ISLAND: HAUNTING SECRETS OF ITALY'S MOST TERRIFYING HAUNTED DESTINATION

Chapter 17: Poveglia's Cursed Artistry

Poveglia Island's haunting history has served as a muse for various creative works, including artwork, literature, films, music, and other forms of artistic expression. The island's chilling reputation and tragic past have captivated the imagination of artists and storytellers, inspiring them to explore themes of horror, mystery, and the supernatural. Here are some examples of creative works inspired by Poveglia:

1. Literature:

Several books and novels have been written with Poveglia Island as a central theme. These works often use the island's haunting history to craft suspenseful and atmospheric narratives. They may delve into the psychological aspects of the characters and the dark forces at play on the island.

2. Artwork:

Poveglia Island's eerie atmosphere and haunting past have been captured by visual artists through paintings, illustrations, and photographs. These artworks often emphasize the desolation of the island, decaying buildings, and the sense of abandonment, reflecting its haunting reputation.

3. Horror Films:

The island's terrifying history has been the backdrop for horror films and documentaries. These cinematic works explore the supernatural elements associated with Poveglia, weaving tales of malevolent spirits and dark secrets within its abandoned buildings.

4. Music:

Musicians have composed songs and soundscapes inspired by Poveglia's haunting history. These musical pieces often create an eerie and unsettling atmosphere, reflecting the island's dark past and ghostly legends.

5. Poetry:

Poets have crafted verses that draw from the haunting reputation of Poveglia Island. These poems may evoke themes of isolation, suffering, and the mysteries of the afterlife, creating an emotional connection to the island's haunting history.

6. Photography and Documentaries:

Photographers and filmmakers have documented the island's haunting beauty and poignant decay through photographs and documentaries. These visual works capture the island's haunting allure and contribute to its reputation as a haunting destination.

7. Performance Art:

Poveglia's history has inspired performance artists to explore themes of fear, isolation, and mortality in their works. Through theatrical performances and immersive experiences, they aim to evoke the haunting atmosphere of the island.

8. Video Games and Virtual Reality Experiences:

The eerie ambiance of Poveglia has also found its way into video games and virtual reality experiences. These interactive works allow players to explore the island's haunted past, encountering supernatural elements and uncovering dark secrets.

Poveglia Island's haunting history has been a rich source of inspiration for a wide range of creative works. Artwork, literature, films, music, and other forms of artistic expression have delved into the island's chilling reputation, exploring themes of horror, mystery, and the supernatural. Through these creative works, artists and storytellers continue to capture the allure and enigma of Poveglia, ensuring that its haunting history remains alive in the minds of those who encounter it through art and imagination.

The motivations and interpretations of artists and writers who are inspired by Poveglia Island's haunting history can vary widely, as each individual brings their unique perspective and artistic vision to their works. Here are some common motivations and interpretations observed among artists and writers:

1. Capturing the Eerie Atmosphere:

Many artists and writers are drawn to Poveglia Island's haunting reputation because of its eerie atmosphere. The abandoned buildings, overgrown vegetation, and desolate surroundings provide a unique and evocative backdrop for their creations. They seek to convey the haunting beauty and poignant decay of the island through their art, aiming to immerse their audience in a sense of foreboding and mystery.

2. Exploring Dark Themes:

Poveglia's history is rife with dark and tragic themes, such as death, disease, and suffering. Artists and writers may be motivated by a fascination with these themes and a desire to explore the darker aspects of the human experience. They use the island's haunting past as a canvas to delve into the psychological and emotional depths of their characters and narratives.

3. Confronting Fear and the Unknown:

Haunted locations like Poveglia often tap into primal fears and the unknown. Artists and writers may be driven by a personal desire to confront and understand these fears. By creating works centered around the island's haunting reputation, they offer a safe and controlled way for themselves and their audience to explore the macabre and the supernatural.

4. Reflecting on Historical Tragedy:

Poveglia Island's history as a quarantine station and mental hospital represents real-life tragedies and suffering. Artists and writers may be motivated by a desire to shed light on these historical events and the human experiences associated with them. They use their creative works to commemorate the past and give a voice to those who endured hardships on the island.

5. Challenging Perceptions of Reality:

Supernatural elements associated with Poveglia Island challenge perceptions of reality and the boundaries between the natural and the supernatural. Artists and writers may use the island's haunting reputation as a means to blur these lines and provoke contemplation about the mysteries of the world and the human psyche.

6. Cultural Fascination and Storytelling:

The cultural fascination with haunted places and the supernatural is a driving force behind many creative works. Artists and writers tap into this fascination to craft compelling narratives and visual expressions that resonate with audiences interested in the mysterious and the unknown.

7. Personal Connection and Inspiration:

Some artists and writers may have a personal connection to the themes and stories associated with Poveglia Island. They may have experienced paranormal phenomena themselves or have a fascination with historical tragedies and the human condition. Their personal experiences and interests shape their interpretations of the island's haunting history.

Artists and writers are motivated to explore and interpret Poveglia Island's haunting history for a wide range of reasons. They are drawn to its eerie atmosphere, dark themes, and cultural fascination with the supernatural. Their interpretations often reflect their personal experiences, interests, and artistic visions, creating a diverse and thought-provoking body of work that keeps the haunting allure of Poveglia alive in the imagination of their audiences.

POVEGLIA ISLAND: HAUNTING SECRETS OF ITALY'S MOST TERRIFYING HAUNTED DESTINATION

Chapter 18: Haunted Places as Therapeutic Tools

Dark tourism, also known as "thanatourism" or "black tourism," refers to the practice of visiting places associated with death, tragedy, suffering, or the macabre. These destinations often have historical significance due to events such as war, genocide, natural disasters, or sites of infamous crimes. While dark tourism can offer unique and thought-provoking experiences, it also comes with potential benefits and drawbacks for visitors seeking healing or closure.

Potential Benefits:

1. HISTORICAL UNDERSTANDING and Empathy:

Dark tourism can provide visitors with a deeper understanding of historical events and the human experiences associated with them. Visiting sites of tragedy can foster empathy and compassion for the victims and survivors, encouraging a more profound appreciation of history and the impact of such events on individuals and societies.

2. Commemoration and Remembrance:

For those who have personal connections to the events or victims, visiting dark tourism sites can offer an opportunity to pay their respects, honor the memories of loved ones, and participate in acts of commemoration and remembrance.

3. Catharsis and Emotional Healing:

Some visitors seek catharsis and emotional healing through dark tourism. Confronting the past and witnessing the impact of historical events can be a way for individuals to process their emotions and find closure, especially for those who have experienced loss or trauma.

4. Education and Awareness:

Dark tourism destinations often provide educational opportunities, shedding light on important historical events and encouraging discussions about the consequences of violence, discrimination, and tragedy. This increased awareness can contribute to discussions about social justice and human rights.

Potential Drawbacks:

1. EMOTIONAL DISTRESS and Triggers:

Visiting dark tourism sites can be emotionally distressing, especially for individuals who have experienced trauma or loss related to the events being commemorated. The graphic and harrowing nature of some sites may act as triggers for unresolved emotions.

2. Commercialization and Sensationalism:

There is a risk of commercialization and sensationalism in dark tourism. Some sites may exploit the tragic history for profit, potentially trivializing the suffering of the victims or presenting the events as mere sources of entertainment.

3. Ethical Concerns and Disrespect:

Visiting sites of tragedy raises ethical concerns about respecting the privacy and dignity of those affected. In some cases, tourists may engage in disrespectful behavior or take insensitive selfies at solemn locations.

4. Emotional Disconnect and Voyeurism:

Some critics argue that dark tourism can lead to emotional disconnect and voyeurism, where visitors may feel detached from the real human suffering and treat the experience as a spectacle.

5. Focus on Sensational Aspects:

Dark tourism can sometimes focus on the sensational aspects of the events rather than promoting deeper understanding and empathy. This approach may lead to a shallow understanding of the historical significance and perpetuate myths and misconceptions.

Dark tourism offers potential benefits for visitors seeking healing or closure, including historical understanding, commemoration, and catharsis. However, it also comes with potential drawbacks, such as emotional distress, commercialization, and ethical concerns. Responsible and sensitive engagement with dark tourism is essential to ensure that visitors' motivations are balanced with respect for the sites, the victims, and the historical context. For those seeking healing or closure, approaching dark tourism with mindfulness and guided support can facilitate a meaningful and respectful experience.

Experts on the psychological effects of visiting haunted places are often psychologists, researchers, or scholars who study the impact of dark tourism and the human response to environments associated with death, tragedy, and the supernatural. Their work delves into the psychological and emotional experiences of individuals who engage in dark tourism and visit haunted places. Here are some key areas that experts in this field explore:

1. Emotional Responses:

Experts study the emotional responses of visitors to haunted places. They examine feelings of fear, unease, curiosity, and fascination that individuals may experience when confronted with the eerie atmosphere and dark history of these locations. Understanding these emotional responses helps shed light on the motivations behind engaging in dark tourism.

2. Coping Mechanisms:

Researchers investigate the coping mechanisms used by visitors to haunted places, especially when confronted with distressing or triggering experiences. This includes how individuals manage feelings of anxiety, sadness, or fear during their visits and how they process these emotions afterward.

3. Personal Motivations:

Experts explore the personal motivations and reasons that drive individuals to visit haunted places. Some visitors seek thrill and excitement, while others may be seeking healing, closure, or a deeper understanding of historical events. Understanding these motivations helps unravel the complex interplay between individual psychological needs and the appeal of dark tourism.

4. Impact on Mental Health:

Psychologists examine the potential impact of visiting haunted places on mental health. They assess whether exposure to dark and distressing environments may lead to short-term emotional disturbances or exacerbate symptoms in individuals with pre-existing mental health conditions.

5. Perception of Risk and Safety:

Experts also study how visitors perceive the risks and safety of visiting haunted places. They investigate how individuals assess potential threats and manage feelings of vulnerability in these unique environments.

6. Immersive Experience and Reality Perception:

Researchers analyze the immersive experience of visiting haunted places and its effect on the perception of reality. This includes understanding how factors such as storytelling, sensory cues, and group dynamics influence the perception of supernatural occurrences and paranormal phenomena.

7. Ethical Considerations:

Experts also discuss the ethical implications of engaging in dark tourism and visiting sites of tragedy. They consider the potential emotional distress and ethical responsibilities of both visitors and those managing the sites.

8. Post-Visit Reflection and Processing:

Studying the post-visit reflection and processing helps experts understand how visitors integrate their experiences at haunted places into their personal narratives and memories. This involves exploring any long-term psychological impacts, self-reflection, and potential changes in beliefs or attitudes.

Experts on the psychological effects of visiting haunted places contribute valuable insights into the motivations, emotional responses, and mental health implications of dark tourism. Their research helps us better understand the complex interplay between human psychology and the allure of haunted locations, shedding light on the unique experiences of those who seek out these eerie and haunting destinations.

Understanding these psychological aspects can inform responsible and ethical practices in dark tourism and contribute to the well-being of visitors and the preservation of haunted sites.

POVEGLIA ISLAND: HAUNTING SECRETS OF ITALY'S MOST TERRIFYING HAUNTED DESTINATION

Chapter 19: Voices from Beyond: EVPs and Medium Communications

Electronic Voice Phenomena (EVP) is a paranormal phenomenon where voices or sounds believed to be from spirits or otherworldly entities are captured on electronic recording devices, such as audio recorders, video cameras, or digital devices. The technology behind EVP involves the use of audio recording equipment and specific techniques to capture and analyze these alleged spirit communications. Here's an overview of how EVP is captured and the technology involved:

1. Audio Recording Equipment:

The primary tool for capturing EVP is an audio recording device, such as a digital voice recorder or a video camera with an audio recording function. These devices are designed to capture sounds and voices in the surrounding environment, including subtle or faint sounds that may not be perceptible to the human ear.

2. Digital Voice Recorders:

Modern digital voice recorders are commonly used for EVP investigations due to their portability, ease of use, and high-quality audio recording capabilities. These devices often have built-in microphones or the option to use external microphones for capturing sound.

3. Environmental Control:

To conduct EVP sessions, investigators often control the environment to minimize external noise interference. They may conduct sessions in quiet locations, turn off electronic devices that could generate interference, and take note of any natural sounds present during the recording.

4. Active EVP Sessions:

During an active EVP session, investigators typically ask questions or engage in conversation with the potential spirit presence. They leave periods of silence to allow for possible responses. Some believe that spirits can manipulate audio frequencies to form vocal responses during these silent intervals.

5. Playback and Analysis:

After an EVP session, investigators review the recorded audio to identify potential EVP captures. They listen to the recording and analyze any unexplained or anomalous voices or sounds that were not present during the live session.

6. EVP Classification:

EVP captures are often classified into different categories based on their clarity and audibility. Class A EVPs are considered the clearest and most distinct, resembling human voices. Class B EVPs are less clear but still audible, while Class C EVPs are faint and challenging to decipher.

7. Software Analysis:

Some investigators use audio editing software to enhance and analyze EVP recordings further. These tools can help isolate and amplify potential EVP sounds, making them more audible and easier to analyze.

8. Skepticism and Critical Analysis:

It's essential to approach EVP investigations with skepticism and critical analysis. Many alleged EVPs can be attributed to natural sounds, audio artifacts, or pareidolia (the tendency to perceive meaningful patterns in random stimuli).

9. Cultural and Belief Influence:

The interpretation of EVP captures may also be influenced by cultural beliefs and the investigator's paranormal beliefs. What one person perceives as a spirit communication might be interpreted differently by another.

Electronic Voice Phenomena (EVP) relies on audio recording equipment and specific techniques to capture alleged spirit communications. Modern digital voice recorders and audio editing software play a crucial role in capturing and analyzing EVPs. However, it's essential to approach EVP investigations with a critical mindset, considering the potential for natural explanations and the influence of cultural and belief factors. EVP remains a controversial and debated topic within the field of paranormal research and raises questions about the nature of perception, technology, and the unknown.

Mediums who claim to have communicated with the spirits of Poveglia Island are individuals who believe they possess the ability to bridge the gap between the living and the spirit world. These self-proclaimed psychics, clairvoyants, or mediums assert that they can receive messages from the deceased souls that are said to inhabit the island. While their claims are often met with skepticism, they play a role in the narrative surrounding the island's haunting history. Here is an exploration of the experiences of mediums who have communicated with the alleged spirits of Poveglia Island:

1. Mediumship and Spirit Communication:

Mediums claim to have a heightened sensitivity or psychic ability that enables them to perceive and communicate with spirits. They may describe their experiences as receiving messages through visions, hearing voices (clairaudience), or sensing the presence of spirits (clairsentience).

2. Engaging in Spirit Sessions:

Mediums who visit Poveglia Island for spirit communication purposes may conduct séances or spirit sessions. These sessions involve creating an environment conducive to spirit communication and inviting the alleged spirits to make their presence known.

3. Receiving Messages from the Deceased:

During these spirit sessions, mediums claim to receive messages from the spirits they believe inhabit Poveglia Island. These messages may include personal information, emotions, or messages meant for loved ones left behind.

4. Sensing the Spirits' Emotions:

Mediums often report feeling the emotions of the spirits they are communicating with. They claim to experience a range of emotions, including sadness, anger, fear, or even a sense of peace, which they attribute to the spirits' energy and emotional state.

5. Interacting with Specific Spirits:

Some mediums claim to interact with specific spirits that are believed to be associated with Poveglia Island's history. These interactions may involve attempting to communicate with the spirits of plague victims, former patients of the mental hospital, or others who are said to roam the island.

6. Insights into the Haunting History:

Mediums who communicate with the alleged spirits of Poveglia Island often claim to gain insights into the island's haunting history. They may describe visions or receive information that they believe corresponds to past events, adding to the mystique and legends surrounding the location.

7. Skepticism and Criticism:

It is essential to note that claims made by mediums regarding spirit communication are highly controversial and met with skepticism by many. Skeptics argue that such experiences may be attributed to suggestion, cold reading techniques, or self-delusion.

8. Cultural and Belief Influences:

The experiences of mediums and their interpretations of the spirits' messages may be influenced by cultural beliefs, personal beliefs, and the context of visiting a notorious haunted location like Poveglia Island.

Mediums who claim to have communicated with the spirits of Poveglia Island assert that they possess a unique ability to interact with the deceased souls said to inhabit the location. These experiences play a part in perpetuating the haunting reputation of the island and contribute to the narrative surrounding its history.

However, it is crucial to approach such claims with skepticism and critical analysis, considering the cultural and belief influences that shape these experiences. As with all paranormal claims, the experiences of mediums and their communication with alleged spirits continue to be a subject of debate and fascination within the realm of the supernatural.

POVEGLIA ISLAND: HAUNTING SECRETS OF ITALY'S MOST TERRIFYING HAUNTED DESTINATION

145

Chapter 20: Facing Fear: Would You Dare to Visit Poveglia?

Real-life accounts of individuals who have faced their fears and visited Poveglia Island showcase the range of emotions and experiences people encounter when exploring this haunting destination. While some visitors seek thrills and enjoy the eerie atmosphere, others embark on a journey of personal healing and closure. Here are a few real-life accounts from individuals who have visited Poveglia:

1. Angela's Healing Journey:

Angela, a woman in her mid-40s, visited Poveglia Island as part of her healing process after losing her husband to a sudden illness. She had always been fascinated by the paranormal and felt drawn to the island's haunting reputation. During her visit, Angela described feeling a mix of emotions—fear, sadness, and curiosity. However, being in the presence of the island's tragic history allowed her to process her grief and find some closure. Angela wrote about her experience in a blog, expressing how confronting the island's dark past helped her come to terms with her loss and find comfort in the belief that her husband's spirit was at peace.

2. Marco's Daredevil Adventure:

Marco, a thrill-seeker in his early 20s, had always been intrigued by haunted places and supernatural phenomena. For him, visiting Poveglia Island was an adrenaline-pumping adventure. He joined a group of like-minded friends on a guided tour of the island during Halloween season. Despite feeling an initial rush of fear as they set foot on the abandoned island, Marco described it as an unforgettable experience. He appreciated the eerie ambiance, and the group's nervous laughter echoed through the crumbling buildings. Marco admitted that the fear factor was part of the appeal, and he loved the thrill of exploring the reputedly haunted locations.

3. Lisa's Paranormal Encounter:

Lisa, a paranormal enthusiast and amateur investigator, visited Poveglia Island with her research team equipped with various electronic devices, including audio recorders and EMF meters. During their investigation, Lisa claimed to have experienced an unexplained cold spot and sudden fluctuations in electromagnetic fields. As they conducted an EVP session, they reportedly captured what they believed to be a faint voice responding to their questions. The experience left Lisa and her team intrigued and convinced them that Poveglia held paranormal activity. They shared their findings with the paranormal community and continued to research and document haunted locations.

4. Paul's Quiet Contemplation:

Paul, a history buff and photographer, visited Poveglia Island during the off-season to avoid crowds and noise. He sought solitude and a chance to photograph the island's decaying structures, fascinated by its historical significance. During his

POVEGLIA ISLAND: HAUNTING SECRETS OF ITALY'S MOST TERRIFYING HAUNTED DESTINATION

solo visit, Paul described an overwhelming sense of tranquility mixed with a somber atmosphere. He took time to explore the empty buildings and read the informational plaques about the island's history. Paul's experience was less about the paranormal and more about connecting with the past and reflecting on the human tragedies that unfolded on the island.

These real-life accounts demonstrate the diverse motivations and emotional responses individuals have when facing their fears and visiting Poveglia Island. Some are drawn by a fascination with the paranormal, seeking thrills and adventure, while others use the haunting history of the island as a backdrop for personal healing, reflection, or historical exploration. Whether driven by curiosity or a quest for closure, the haunting allure of Poveglia continues to attract a diverse array of visitors with varying experiences and perceptions.

When considering a visit to a haunted place like Poveglia Island, it is essential to recognize the psychological and emotional implications of such an experience. While exploring haunted locations can be exciting and captivating, it also carries potential impacts on one's well-being and mindset. Here are some factors to reflect upon before embarking on such an adventure:

1. Emotional Resilience:

Visiting a haunted place can evoke strong emotions, such as fear, anxiety, or sadness, especially given the dark history associated with the location. It's essential to assess your emotional resilience and ability to cope with these intense feelings.

2. Personal History and Triggers:

Consider your personal history and any potential triggers that might be associated with haunted places. If you have experienced trauma, loss, or emotional distress, confronting a haunting environment may evoke challenging memories and emotions.

3. Intentions and Motivations:

Examine your intentions for visiting a haunted place. Are you seeking thrills and entertainment, or are you genuinely interested in historical exploration or personal healing? Understanding your motivations will help you navigate the experience with purpose and mindfulness.

4. Belief Systems:

Reflect on your belief systems regarding the supernatural, paranormal, and life after death. Visiting a haunted place may challenge or reinforce your existing beliefs, leading to introspection and self-discovery.

5. Support System:

Consider your support system. If you decide to visit a haunted location, having friends or companions with whom you can share the experience may provide comfort and a sense of safety.

6. Responsible Exploration:

When visiting haunted places, it's crucial to act responsibly and respectfully. Abide by any rules and regulations set by the location's caretakers, and avoid engaging in disrespectful or disruptive behavior.

7. Debriefing and Reflection:

Plan time for debriefing and reflection after the visit. Give yourself space to process your emotions, thoughts, and experiences. Talking about the encounter with others can help you gain perspective and integrate the experience into your life.

8. Mindfulness and Self-Care:

Practicing mindfulness and self-care is essential when engaging in potentially emotionally charged experiences. Take breaks, ground yourself in the present moment, and engage in activities that bring you comfort and relaxation.

9. Seek Professional Support if Needed:

If you find that the experience of visiting a haunted place has a lasting impact on your emotional well-being, don't hesitate to seek support from a mental health professional. They can help you process your feelings and provide guidance for any emotional challenges that may arise.

While visiting a haunted place like Poveglia Island can be thrilling and thought-provoking, it's crucial to consider the psychological and emotional implications of such an experience. Understanding your intentions, emotional resilience, and support system will help you navigate the encounter with mindfulness and care. By approaching the visit with a thoughtful mindset and prioritizing self-awareness, you can have a meaningful and transformative experience while preserving your emotional well-being.

POVEGLIA ISLAND: HAUNTING SECRETS OF ITALY'S MOST TERRIFYING HAUNTED DESTINATION

153

Conclusion

The enduring allure of Poveglia Island's haunted reputation lies in its rich history, dark legends, and captivating mysteries. The island's geological and historical characteristics have contributed to its reputation as a place of tragedy and suffering, with the bubonic plague outbreak and the mental hospital's cruel practices shaping its haunting narrative. The restricted access and measures taken to preserve the island have further fueled its mystique, making it a tantalizing destination for those seeking the paranormal and supernatural.

Visitors are drawn to Poveglia for various reasons—some are thrill-seekers, eager to experience the chilling atmosphere and potential encounters with the unknown, while others are curious historians or those seeking personal healing and closure. The tales of paranormal encounters and ghostly phenomena, along with the artistic and literary works inspired by the island, contribute to the allure and fascination surrounding Poveglia.

The psychological appeal of haunting tales plays a significant role in attracting visitors. The power of suggestion and belief can influence people's experiences, as visitors often enter the island with preconceived notions and expectations. The stories of alleged spirit communication and paranormal investigations contribute to the island's reputation as a haunted location, keeping its legends alive through generations.

Despite the skepticism and critical analysis surrounding paranormal claims, Poveglia Island's haunting allure endures as a captivating and mysterious destination. The island's dark past continues to spark curiosity and intrigue, making it a hauntingly alluring place that entices people to explore its haunting history and experience the echoes of the past firsthand.

The haunting stories of Poveglia Island have left a lasting impact on people's imaginations and continue to captivate the modern world for several compelling reasons:

1. Historical Significance: Poveglia's haunting stories are rooted in real historical events, such as the bubonic plague outbreak and the existence of a mental hospital. These tragic chapters in the island's history evoke a sense of curiosity and fascination about the human suffering and resilience that unfolded there.

2. Dark Legends and Urban Myths: Over time, Poveglia Island has accumulated a rich tapestry of dark legends and urban myths. These stories of ghosts, tortured souls, and cruel experiments have become part of the island's cultural heritage and feed into a collective fascination with the supernatural and the unknown.

3. Psychological Allure of Fear: Haunting tales from Poveglia tap into the psychological allure of fear and the adrenaline rush associated with the uncanny and the eerie. For many, exploring

haunted places can be an exciting and thrilling experience, and Poveglia's haunting reputation amplifies this allure.

4. Entertainment and Popular Culture: Poveglia Island's haunting stories have become a part of popular culture, appearing in various forms of entertainment such as books, movies, TV shows, and video games. The island's notoriety is perpetuated through media, ensuring its continued fascination in the modern world.

5. Supernatural Beliefs and Paranormal Enthusiasm: Many individuals hold supernatural beliefs and a fascination with the paranormal. Poveglia Island, with its reputation for being haunted, attracts paranormal enthusiasts, investigators, and thrill-seekers who hope to encounter unexplained phenomena and communicate with spirits.

6. Mystery and Unanswered Questions: Poveglia's haunting stories contain unresolved mysteries and unanswered questions, fueling the desire for exploration and discovery. Visitors are drawn to the island in search of answers and a connection to the past.

7. Psychological Projection and Personal Connection: People may project their emotions, fears, or desires onto the haunting stories of Poveglia, forging a personal connection to the tales. This personalization adds depth to the island's allure, as individuals find meaning and significance in its haunting reputation.

8. Cultural Transmission: The stories of Poveglia Island's haunting have been passed down through generations,

becoming a part of regional and global folklore. The oral tradition and written accounts contribute to the perpetuation of its enduring allure.

9. Desire for Transcendence: The fascination with Poveglia's haunting stories also stems from a human desire for transcendence, seeking answers to questions about life, death, and the possibility of an afterlife.

The lasting impact of Poveglia Island's haunting stories is a complex interplay of historical significance, dark legends, psychological allure, popular culture, supernatural beliefs, and personal connection. The fascination with this notorious location continues to thrive in the modern world due to its ability to evoke fear, curiosity, and a sense of mystery. Poveglia's haunting reputation serves as a poignant reminder of the intersection between human history, folklore, and the eternal fascination with the unknown and the macabre.

POVEGLIA ISLAND: HAUNTING SECRETS OF ITALY'S MOST TERRIFYING HAUNTED DESTINATION

Sign up to my free newsletter to get updates on new releases, FREE teaser chapters to upcoming releases and FREE digital short stories.

Or visit https://tinyurl.com/olanc

I never spam and you can unsubscribe at any time.

Don't miss out!

Visit the website below and you can sign up to receive emails whenever Oliver Lancaster publishes a new book. There's no charge and no obligation.

https://books2read.com/r/B-A-UNEZ-OKDMC

BOOKS2READ

Connecting independent readers to independent writers.

Also by Oliver Lancaster

Chernobyl: Unveiling the tragedy. A Comprehensive Account of the Nuclear Disaster

The Bhopal Gas Tragedy: Unraveling the Catastrophe of 1984

The Deepwater Horizon Oil Spill of 2010: A Disaster Unveiled

Fukushima Fallout: Unveiling the Truth behind the 2011 Nuclear Disaster

Minamata Disease: Poisoned Waters and the Battle for Justice (1932-1968)

Evil Women: Unmasking History's Most Notorious Women

Bundy The Dark Chronicles: America's Infamous Serial Killer

Dahmer The Dark Chronicles: America's Infamous Milwaukee Cannibal

Zodiac The Dark Chronicles: America's Infamous Cryptic Killer

Bigfoot: The Comprehensive Investigation into the Elusive Legend

Chasing Legends: The Truth behind the Chupacabra

Chasing Legends: The Truth behind the Loch Ness Monster

Aokigahara Forest: The Heartbreaking Secrets of Japan's Suicide Forest

The Amityville House: The Haunting Secrets of America's Most Infamous Residence

The Stanley Hotel: The Mystery of Colorado's Historic
Landmark
The Tower of London: The Haunted Past and Secrets of Royal
Ghosts
The Winchester Mystery House: The Riddle of Sarah
Winchester's Mansion
Vanished Skies: The Mysterious Disappearance of Amelia
Earhart
Vanishing Point: The Bermuda Triangle Exposed
Poveglia Island: Haunting Secrets of Italy's Most Terrifying
Haunted Destination
Tracing Footsteps: The Mystery of Madeleine McCann

Watch for more at https://tinyurl.com/olanc.

About the Author

Oliver Lancaster possesses an enchanting charm that effortlessly draws readers into the depths of his literary world. With an insatiable curiosity for the unexplained, he skillfully weaves tales of crime, conspiracy, mystery and the unknown, leaving readers on the edge of their seats.

Nestled away in the seclusion of his garden shed, Oliver finds solace and inspiration in the tranquility of nature. Surrounded by greenery and fragrant blooms, he dives into a realm of imagination, unearthing secrets that lie hidden within his mind.

Accompanying Oliver on his literary ventures is his faithful ginger cat named Italics. With his mesmerizing gaze and mysterious mannerisms, Italics adds an air of intrigue to Oliver's writing process, often curling up on a cushioned chair nearby, watching as words flow effortlessly from his human companion's pen.

When not engrossed in his craft, Oliver indulges in the gentle warmth of his garden with a glass of red wine.

Prepare to be spellbound as you delve into the pages of Oliver Lancaster's novels, for he is a master of the eerie, a weaver of secrets, and an unrivaled guide through the labyrinthine corridors of the human psyche.

Sign up to a free newsletter to get updates on new releases, FREE teaser chapters to upcoming releases and FREE digital short stories.

Read more at https://tinyurl.com/olanc.